HADRIAN'S
WALL

HADRIAN'S WALL

ARCHAEOLOGICAL WALKING GUIDES

CLIFFORD JONES

The History Press

Look beneath the surface: never let a thing's intrinsic quality or worth escape you.

— Emperor Marcus Aurelius

Publisher's Note

The views expressed herein are those of the author
and do not necessarily represent those of the publisher.

First published 2012

The History Press
The Mill, Brimscombe Port
Stroud, Gloucestershire, GL5 2QG
www.thehistorypress.co.uk

British Library Cataloguing in Publication Data.
A catalogue record for this book is available from the British Library.

ISBN 978 0 7524 6361 2

Typesetting and origination by The History Press
Printed in Great Britain

CONTENTS

ACKNOWLEDGEMENTS

The author wishes to acknowledge and thank the following people and organisations: Susie Jones, Graham Dicker, Alan Biggins, John Buckland, Jennifer Morrison, Dawn Robinson, the Orlands and the staff of Cumbria County Council Heritage Services, Tyne & Wear Archaeology, the Council for British Archaeology and Timescape Surveys.

PREFACE

When the author was faced with the enviable prospect of writing a guide to Hadrian's Wall a decision had to be made.

Was it to follow the same format as others?

Most definitely not: this author does things differently, not because he disagrees with the approach of others – not at all, there are some excellent works on the subject. Simply he believes there is always a different way of looking at things and Hadrian's Wall is no exception. This is an adventure, with hard–earned fun and a dash of self–fulfilment thrown in for good measure.

It is an exploration, an observation; a personal expedition into the past in the midst of the present. It is not a march from A to Z. You, 'the walker', will be going to forgotten places, some of which will call upon you, get you pondering, wondering and questioning our understanding when you least expect it. They will call you back, tap you on the shoulder and pose challenges to you as to what more can be done to explain their pasts.

You will be in the great classrooms of Cumbria and Northumberland and you will learn in wet, wind and sometimes, if you are blessed, sun. There will be the author's usual and apparent scant regard for health and safety; pronouncements regarding common sense and, where required, precise details of how to find the nearest pub.

There will be mud. Plus, metro trains, tarmac, pavements and the odd bus. Not forgetting happy cows!

Something for everyone …

Enjoy!

1 The Wall: Keeping the barbarians out, or the Romans in?

2 Bewcastle cross detail. A post-Roman world defined in stone

HADRIAN'S WALL WORLD HERITAGE SITE & NATIONAL TRAIL CONSERVATION TIPS

For conservation reasons Hadrian's Wall Path was designated as a footpath only (not for cycling or horse riding) and government approval to use public funds in order to create the route stipulated that, with very few exceptions, it should be managed as a green sward path.

A green sward, or grass path, is important for several reasons. It is considered to be the best way of protecting any archaeology underfoot; it presents the visible archaeology, both masonry and earthworks, in the most sympathetic of settings; and an unbroken grass surface means that farmers' grazing land is respected.

The National Trail's visitor management approach is atypical and unlike any other access or heritage management project in the UK, Europe or possibly beyond. Uniquely, it is promoted as a spring, summer and autumn destination only, not as a winter one.

Long-term Meteorological Office data shows that the World Heritage site's soils are at field capacity, or saturated, from about the end of October to about the end of April. Saturated soils are more easily damaged, thereby rendering the monument vulnerable to erosion, with the potential for loss of the archaeological record. For this reason the trail's popular Passport season operates each year from 1 May to 31 October only, with day or short-break visitors in the winter months encouraged instead to explore the many promoted circular walks in the wider Hadrian's Wall countryside.

With an eye to the future everyone can help to conserve the World Heritage site by following a couple of very simple conservation tips. Visitors should avoid walking on top of the masonry Wall and, by walking side-by-side along the grass path, instead of in single file, they can effectively double its carrying capacity. It really does help to make a positive difference.

www.nationaltrail.co.uk/hadrianswall
www.hadrians-wall.org

INTRODUCTION

AD 122 AND ALL THAT ...

'Hadrian's Wall covers 73 miles across the countryside of the North East and North West and the cities of Newcastle and Carlisle. Internationally celebrated as a World Heritage Site, it is the best known frontier in the Entire Roman Empire. Discover what life was like as a Roman with English Heritage.'

ENGLISH HERITAGE

www.english-heritage.org.uk/daysout/properties/hadrians-wall

Hadrian's Wall is seen as one of the greatest examples of Roman power in the United Kingdom. Its carefully restored stonework brings a glimpse of the past to life. It is packaged and described as a national treasure. It is, but we, the English-speaking people, tend to see the Wall in terms of a singular structure – which it is not. Nor is it quite as it is packaged; it has to be seen in a wider context.

The Emperor Antonine Pius (AD 142) managed to encircle the entire Roman Empire and pushed the British boundary further north (ignoring Hadrian's frontier); it seems a little remiss of English Heritage to put all the emphasis on the one wall rather than on the fact it is part of a something bigger and even more complicated. Hadrian's German 'limes' system is equally well known and in many respects better preserved and interpreted for public display.

Hadrian's Wall, therefore, is not a 'one off'; it should be seen as part of a greater whole. This does not distract from its importance, but merely puts it in its place, especially as there are at least two other Roman frontiers in Britain. These are the Antonine frontier between the Forth and the Clyde, and the Gask frontier in south-west Scotland; there are no doubt another couple that will be seen in the near future as legitimate short-term military frontiers, or the edges to the Roman occupation, or simply a boundary between the Roman tax system and the tax free.

The Wall is fascinating, both for its physical remains and for the reason for its construction. In many ways it makes good sense if you want a means of slowing down an attacking force; it certainly wouldn't stop an invasion, but would allow enough time for forces to be raised to repel such an attack. But who has such an army and if the Romans are aware of such a force it simply was not in the Roman psyche to sit on its haunches and wait for an enemy to attack.

The Roman military machine preferred disciplined demolition of any enemy in high gear, so it is odd to see a frontier with all the comforts of permanency turning up in north-west Britain, taking up effort and resources. It is in contrast to the German limes, which were built apparently to do the exact same thing in a real war zone. They weren't built to anything like the same level of permanency along its entire length, allowing for its very well-built forts.

3 The Wall at Birdoswald

Hadrian seemed determined to identify the north-western limits of the Roman world. This could possibly be the result of a historic uncertainty in respect of Roman expansion dating back to Augustus, having been brought sharply home by his predecessor Trajan's surge into massive imperial expansion to the east. Upon Hadrian's succession this expansion was swiftly stopped as he witnessed an empire stretched beyond its capacity to cope, on the absolute limit of central control. Alternatively, this could be a result of a grand statement of personal insecurity. The answer is utterly unclear. Whatever it is, Hadrian has left his mark, or to be precise his name, for much is not what it may seem and the emperor may well be credited with rather too much of the picture. The canvas is broad and one paintbrush does not cover it all.

THEORIES

The author can confirm that to date nobody has conclusively proven exactly why Hadrian's Wall was actually built. Here are a couple of the author's theories, to add to the many others on offer. Feel free to disagree.

Theory One: Understand the Man, Understand the Wall?

Hadrian undoubtedly had problems: a continual sense of personal worthlessness and paranoia, perhaps of it being found out that he possibly was not entitled to the empire at all – rumours had abounded regarding his predecessor Emperor Marcus Ulpius Nerva Traianus's (Trajan's) will. There is no doubt that Hadrian understood his imperial position was the result of Pompeia Plotina (Trajan's wife) persuading the emperor in his last exhausted days to entrust the empire to him. Hadrian had served by Trajan's side and was fully aware of the military's respect for the old emperor, and of the opportunity his fellow members of the elite had to undermine him; balancing the whole was a key factor in his own personal survival. Plotina's quite flagrant intervention in Roman imperial affairs was not unique – far from it – but her well-intentioned meddling would always tarnish his brilliance. Hadrian's suicide bids, excluding the understandable emotional grief at his lover Antinus' death, seem to relate to an inner voice – the grander the external display, the deeper his sense of personal loss. The wagging tongues could be executed; the ones in his head could not.

Due to Trajan's military efforts the Roman Empire had grown enormous and was on the brink of being unmanageable; Hadrian could negotiate boundaries with his neighbours with the advantage of might. Hadrian had been on the spot with Trajan and knew he had the upper hand, but the cost wasn't worth the effort. Stabilising the economy (no longer on a continual expansionist war footing), as well as extracting allegiances and trade deals with those that he freed from recent Roman control, allowed him to veil his internal angst by portraying the opposite: grand public works. Hadrian would not be the first or last emperor to use this means to placate his enemies, by public show. The problem for Hadrian, an intelligent, astute and artistic individual, was a deep-set self-doubt within himself.

Hadrian devised some truly incredible imperial works which, by the nature of their scale, kept the generals, their troops and thus the economy busy. These were undoubtedly deliberate distractions developed to balance out the fact that Trajan had inadvertently weighted the balance of power, not in the Senate or the emperor, but in the generals. The Trajanic gains for the Roman Empire were so huge that, upon Trajan's death, the empire could quite easily have imploded, with generals fighting to become emperor. The author believes that Plotina foresaw this possibility and put Hadrian in command to prevent a potential civil war; she had a clear understanding of Roman politics and had more than once demonstrated her abilities to keep the populace happy. There would have been an opportunity for her to have had direct dialogue with Hadrian in advance of Trajan's death through Sabina, Hadrian's estranged wife (Hadrian having no heterosexual inclinations) and Trajan's great niece. Hadrian was in charge of the army in the east at the time and his very first act was to give away all the eastern gains so as to concentrate on complete command of the empire at its core. Sabina, tending the soon-to-be-dead emperor, may well have been close enough to hear the conversations of the generals before they offered their respects.

This urgency indicates a keen understanding of the political atmosphere and plays a part in the subsequent imperial rule. An emperor cannot be everywhere – though Hadrian does a very good impression of being so; if he were not the wheels might have come off the imperial wagon. This touring and external show has all the makings of hype, because behind the scenes Hadrian was a man who was so would routinely order a temporary fort to be built inside the existing fort he was visiting, and when at home lived on a small island in his own palace.

Hadrian needed to keep the machinery of government busy, locked into building projects, which indirectly locked everyone in – like himself.

Theory Two: A Furtherance of Theory One

Hadrian understood the army; he thus saw it as to his benefit to employ a programme of competitive spirit within the military through the frontier-building programme (not just in north-west Britain, but Germany as well), each legion competing against each other to build the best. Activity, manual effort, keeps the troops busy; busy troops are happy because they are working and not being shot at by an enemy: they are simply building a wall, digging a vallum (rampart), cutting a tree down, which is much better than being stabbed at by a barbarian, and happy troops don't have reasons for grievances against their emperor. However, there is a downside to all this building, which will be discussed anon.

Is this relative delight in a construction project by the troops the result of some need for relaxation after a great number of military losses?

There are some slightly dubious comments in the historical records suggesting that all was not sweetness and light in Britain during the early years of Hadrian's reign. One Marcus Cornelius Fronto, orator, rhetorician and grammarian (not a historian, as others may wish to describe him) suggests to Emperor Marcus Aurelius that Hadrian had indeed had difficulties in Britain during his reign:

> …what great numbers of soldiers were killed by the Jews, what great numbers by the Britons …
>
> Fronto, *Parthian War*, 2, 220

It must be understood that any losses Hadrian had were nothing compared to the troubles of Aurelius. Fronto was (when the full context of the work is taken into account) merely trying to make the best of a difficult situation faced by Aurelius and, frankly, failing in doing so.

The Parthian Wars (ad 114–5), to which Fronto is alluding, do not represent Rome's finest hour; indeed, Trajan probably died as a result of the exertion and there was considerable conflict with the Jews in all the territories concerned, down to the Persian Gulf which spread to Cyprus, Cyrene and Egypt. Hadrian, in military command of the forces in Parthia at the time of Trajan's death, had to settle the whole inglorious campaign; which he promptly did by settling with the Parthians, decimating the Jews and heading back to Rome.

The second occasion Hadrian had to deal with the Jews was in the Bar-Kokhba revolt, which started in ad 123 with a series of attacks and only turned into a full-scale conflict in ad 132, when the Shimon Bar-Kokhba seized Jerusalem. Hadrian sent 12 legions and whilst there were heavy casualties, the nation of Judea disappeared from the map to become Syria Palestina. Neither of these events really fit the bill for Britain during Hadrian's imperium – there is no major archaeological record of a revolt on such a scale.

INTRODUCTION

One thing Fronto does show is that Hadrian was quite capable of commanding vast armies and completely removing an enemy, or alternatively seeing the futility of the situation and coming to terms – nothing if not pragmatic. Neither scenario really fits the principle of a wall for Britain; possibly for Germany where the Romans had a long history of attempted northern control, going back to Augustus at the start of the imperial age.

There is little to dispute that Hadrian made sure he was extremely obvious to his troops (he needed to stay alive); indeed, he is seen as popular (which meant it worked); such a 'cult of personality' was implicit in the role. Some emperors employed the 'look at me, I embody the great worth of the Empire' approach better than others, yet it was a vital part of the job. How this 'imperial' personality played upon Hadrian's internal mental state (there can be no worse threat to the mental stability of those that feel internally worthless than having no choice but to accept the acclamation of others) can only be witnessed in the last few years of his reign, when the paranoia, attendant mental instability, grief and suicidal tendencies gained the upper hand. Quite possibly, the effort required to keep the whole machine of empire working had left him exhausted; death would have felt like a rest.

The Wall in northern Britain can be viewed as not for keeping people out, but to keep people in: locked into a system that is trying to stabilise itself, coming to terms with the physical enormity and prosperity of the land and people it administers and controls, and quite possibly locked into the personal fears of one man. This distant corner was as far away from Rome and Roman politics as it was possible to get. The only people present were there at imperial request, dutifully building a physical manifestation of their emperor's emotional prison.

This guide will not tell you everything about the Wall, because, as has been discussed, there is no conclusive argument as to its actual singular purpose from its conception. Whilst we do understand its continued use, and oft as not uselessness, the Wall offers more questions than answers. This provides the walker room for theory and personal speculation and is one of the most remarkable Roman archaeological enigmas in Europe.

Let us breakdown some walls to start with.

This guide will concentrate on the east to west and most readily recognised frontier, which we call 'Hadrian's Wall'. It should be noted that most of what is on display to the public is post-Hadrianic, rebuilding and refurbishment works, as you would expect for a structure that saw 300 years of military use and 1000 years of reuse; though it would be unfair to say there are no Hadrianic works to view.

The frontier goes further than Kirkbride; it heads down the Cumbrian coast to Ravenglass, another hundred-odd miles when the estuaries of the west coast are taken into account. Effectively you are halfway along the frontier when you reach Bowness-on-Solway.

The route from Ravenglass to Bowness-on-Solway is covered in the author's Walking Hadrian's Coastal Route (The History Press, 2008). This gives the other half an airing and only goes to emphasise the scale of Hadrian's grand plan.

The Wall provides a barrier, even if it is a relatively fragile one, with a hole in it between Wallsend and Tynemouth. The conundrum of the 'gap' opens up a world of theoretical possibilities as to the Wall's purpose and potential of the archaeology.

The Wall infrastructure also poses some thorny issues, such as milecastles being where they should not and vice versa; turrets and towers missing from the strict military-engineering regime; width of walls changing and works being shifted; and half-completed works left because they were too difficult (according to some). These all make for a far from straightforward picture, which is why the author is wary of presenting a 'we know Hadrian's Wall' picture – we don't. Far from it. In all aspects we are still in the dark because the evidence has not yet been thoroughly interrogated, because of the lack of excavation.

THE WALL: KNOWN WORKS

- **120km – length of wall east to west**
- **17 known forts and major military sites, probably more**
- **c.80 milecastles**
- **65 construction camps**

Some of the above are reasonably understood; the majority not. Plus the myriad of sites not properly recorded or recorded so poorly we might as well be starting again. Milecastle and turret numbering is a nightmare and is not for the faint hearted. The author suggests trying to theorise using the number – that way madness lies. Especially as we really cannot be sure as to what is actually present along the entire length, nor is the numbering sequence of any ancient importance – it is merely a modern method of trying to understand. However, doing this accidently imposes constraints, as if we really do know all there is.

'Hello Sextus – I've just been up to milecastle XXII to do a plastering job, right next door there's that odd turret XVI; nothing like turret XXIV; cor, you can see the difference. Those lads in the Auguata II Hispana don't half do a good job.'

I think not.

The undisputable core factor is the landscape: here is the bedrock (save for some nibbling at it in the way of quarries), a constant, above speculation. The frontier uses landscape to its advantage; the engineers took decisions based on the highs and lows, the rivers and the points of crossing and what they could provide to the advantage of the imperial design.

Visibility is a core ingredient – a case of 'in your face pal' if ever there was one; covert it is not.

Imagine a long, high wall, stretching as far as the eye can see; painted white, shining brightly, the red horizontals and verticals of painted stonework in stark contrast to the white, emphasising accuracy and attention to detail. Below, the neatly trimmed grass, with a gravel path at its base, not a stone daring to be out of place; the occasional stone inscription, painted yellow, green and red (for maximum visibility), set into the banks of the vallum (rampart), identifying the legion responsible for its construction – a scene of military perfection.

During Hadrian's reign there was only one major rebellion recorded for the military to deal with (at Judea: the Bar Kokhbar revolt). This is nothing in comparison with Trajan's activities – instead, any potential or existing action was curtailed by diplomacy (such as at Parthia). This meant there were a larger number of troops available. Hadrian was unlikely to suggest reducing the forces because the empire needed policing and any reduction would be very bad for his health. The generals, all considering their political careers, would have needed to prove they were useful to the emperor in non-direct militaristic terms. A major civil engineering project, ordered by the emperor, was a good way to get ahead.

The Wall becomes an advertisement of personal worth and there is no shortage of advertising of worth along the Wall; units and individuals left their nearly indelible mark all over the place. This is a conscious act of self-promotion.

'Look what I have done – can I have a promotion?'

Significantly for us all, the following inscription, probably from milecastle 38, assists in nailing Hadrian to the Wall (for many years it was thought a later emperor, Severus, built it) and the mention of Nepos gives us the date AD 122:

IMP CAES TRAIAN HADRIANA AUG LEG II AUG A PLATORIO
NEPOTE LEG PR PR

To the emperor Caesar Trajan Hadrian Augustus, the Second Legion Augusta (built this)
for Aulus Platorius Nepos, his pro-praetorian Legate

Great works, so well recorded would certainly have looked the part, but to the author it is more a sign of a military in denial. There is no flexibility – stone is by its nature set – plus the practicality of a stone wall is an option when the walker the time and safety to build it. It indicates a disturbing reality, a limit to Roman military might, which was certainly not lost on those building it. The military would have been happy with the turf and wood frontier (the Western Wall started as such) because there was a good chance this would be abandoned and the army would march on. The change in command to stone would have made it crystal clear what the message was to the troops.

Such building activities, the physical quarrying of stone, earthworks and forestry clearance, required a fed workforce. This in turn led to a series of agricultural industries arising, a mixture of local tribal enterprise and Romans seizing opportunities as they came about leaving marks on the landscape, be they roads, potteries, field systems, or cattle enclosures. This activity was not all south of the Wall; there were plenty of established Roman goings-on deep beyond it. These hidden places are as important as the Wall itself; indeed, they provide clues to aid our understanding of it.

The Wall, constructed between AD 122 and 126, saw little or no military conflict; indeed, it was retired until AD 155, when the Antonine frontier was temporarily out of use, then again sporadically through AD 181–4, when the locals to the north got a little out of hand. There was subsequent rebuilding of parts in AD 205. There was then nothing of any consequence until AD 343, when things turned very nasty indeed, but with a good patch-up all continued reasonably well until 367, when it took another substantial hit. Fortunately, order was just about restored, whilst the Roman Empire eventually turned its back on Britain with a quick imperial 'Sorry lads you're on your own' from the hard-pressed Emperor Honorius. However, the Wall never went completely out of use, providing bases for local leaders of a post-Roman world; subsequently the forts became strongholds for cattle thieves (reivers), especially in the central region, and as a result of nobody willing to attempt to quarry stone from the Wall in such a dangerous spot. The reivers, seeing that the game was up when King James VI of Scotland inherited the English throne, legitimised some of their activity with limestone quarrying and small-scale farming, all centred on the same sites. New roads across the zone were constructed for military purposes, but they soon became conduits for landowners to set up model tenanted farms. The Wall saw more damage from these landowners than ever it did from those from the north. Fortunately, its worth as a remnant of another age was recognised and it is still in use today as a major tourist attraction. One day we might fully understand it!

It is the physicality, the fact the stones tell of the people who built it, the effort, the sweat, the noise, that we all should seek. Not a name, not one man – he is only one name in a very long and complicated story.

Hadrian's Wall, product of one man's paranoia and a military sideshow.
Or:
Hadrian's Wall, the result of a massive Roman disaster as suggested by Fronto (for which we have no evidence).

The walker can decide, or there again not; there is no obligation to do so. Theory is good fun, but better with a few hard facts to back it up. Just enjoy the view; the rest will come with the doing. A theory will creep up behind the walker without warning, take hold and enlighten the evening in the pub no end; especially if there is a counter-argument and the ale particularly good!

The walker thus provided with the author's theory can now proceed to knock it down, stamp all over it and start again.

Much that the walker will see is a conglomerate; mostly post-Hadrian, save for the Wall itself. The Wall has survived many stages of use, misuse and abandonment; it presents itself better now than it has in over 1000 years. It is recognised for its historic importance and is cared for; it has a definite presence – if the walker is alone with it they will understand. Just stand, enjoy the view and let it do its work; battered it maybe, but it is not dead.

The author is as guilty as everyone else of attributing the site to one person; it should be attributed to the silent shadows of the thousands of men and women who lived, loved, fought and died within its shadow. They are the true owners of the Wall through their efforts. That is why he calls it 'the Wall'.

So for Hadrian read the unsung champions, the people.

Hadrian's Wall World Heritage Site

- Tempting though it may be, do not stand on or climb the Wall.
- Follow the guide paths to prevent erosion.
- Report any damage at the earliest opportunity – early intervention prevents further distress.

Please avoid walking or climbing on Hadrian's Wall

It is a fragile and sensitive monument and is easily damaged

4 Hadrian's Wall perfection – well nearly if it were complete

AN ALTERNATIVE VIEW OF THE WALL'S ORIGIN & PURPOSE

Prototype

There is some archaeological evidence to suggest the western part of the Wall, especially between Bowness-on-Solway (possibly even Kirkbride) and Corbridge, had an early defensive frontier system. This was to protect Roman interests from the tribes beyond the Solway and the tribes of the north-east, in particular, to the north, the Selgovae tribe occupying the area immediately across the Solway and, to a lesser extent, the Novantae occupying the peninsula of Galloway to the far north-west. There is good reason to believe that the Solway was a very flexible boundary with ample opportunity to raid for cattle, slaves and general goods. The Carvetii on the south bank were no doubt equally keen to acquire the Selgovae possessions to the north in return. So it appears to have been a relative stalemate, one for which both sides had probably agreed terms, and the site of Carlisle is an agreed tribal outcome – a place to trade at a bridging point.

The arrival of formal Roman military influence with Quintus Petillius Cerialis in AD 71 and, shortly after, Gnaues Julius Agricola in AD 77 might well have caused some concern to all parties. However, the Carvetii seemed to respond well to the initial Roman advance, as well as appearing to keep out of the Brigantes' civil war (their neighbours to the east), which the Cerealis had exploited to good effect. The Roman occupying power seem to have been accepted as friendly senior allies as this took the strain off relations with the pro-Roman part of the Brigantes and put the Carvetii in a strong position with their northern neighbours.

Any Roman general worth his salt would recognise the exposed area from Bowness-on-Solway to Carlisle could be a very dangerous place; the Carvetii would have added a list of events that would confirm this. There was a need for the Romans to take some defensive action as they were amassing forces and supplies for engagements further north, and these would be obvious with the activity up and down the Cumbrian coast. The temptation for incursions by raiding parties to rustle cattle and horses was recognised and a series of ditches, palisades and towers would dissuade such enthusiastic tourism.

This basic system of towers and works advanced up the Solway as required. Not a continual line, but merely a strongpoint where required; visibility was the key. They may not have been continually manned which would have kept the potential raiders guessing as to where the Romans were. This system runs to the timber fort at Carlisle and across the River Eden to the site of Stanwix and ultimately along what became the Stanegate (Roman road) to Castlestead and Brampton and then Gilsland beyond, but not along the present wall course. The towers, ditches, camps and forts were temporary; merely part of a standard Roman military way of making sure they prevail over the local landscape and population. Strategic parts of this network survived the intervening years between the late AD 70s and 100s, becoming part of a permanent barrier, but for reasons other than fear of incursions.

This prototype frontier of occasional strategic towers and road system would have made its way to Corbridge and then headed north to Chesters; from which it headed out into the wilds of Northumberland, deep into Votandi territory to Swine Hill NY9082 and then across to Longshaws NZ135885; Learchild (Aluana); Chew Green NT7808; Oxton NT4954; Elginhaugh NT3267; Cramond NT1976; terminating at Borrowstounness NT0280 (Velviniate). This thus encompasses a vast swathe of productive land and the major tribal military and civilian settlements to the east, establishing an overview of the Firth of Forth within Roman control. By doing so it provided invaluable grain reserves for the Roman army and an apparent compliant workforce. Road systems were constructed to move grain and goods, and river crossings and bridges protected. Most of this system, in one form or another, would have still been in place over 30 years later to allow Hadrian to rationalise it into a straightforward east–west route with a revision to dealings with the north.

A north-eastern annexation would have been a useful tool around AD 70, when the Brigantes were rebelling against their leader (client ruler) Cartimandua, protecting Roman access to the Tyne and preventing the two tribes from getting together by placing a sizeable wedge between the two. The Romans had to rescue the pro-Roman Cartimandua, so the situation was serious enough. The emperor Vespasian (AD 69–79) had enough of the Brigantes problem and simply removed the client kingdom status. Allowing for the bubbling problem of the Brigantes royal house, Vespasian probably recognised that Rome had nominal control from York to Edinburgh as a result of work already done and the kingdom was surplus to Rome's requirements.

The archaeology is there, especially camps and some minor works – it's simply a case of putting the pieces together and looking more closely at the landscape between the forts; the vestiges of ditches; potential tower bases; the odd vallum. Who knows what lies below the sod?

Time will tell and you the walker can be part of it.

GETTING INVOLVED IN ARCHAEOLOGY

The desire to explore, to know why, or simply to enjoy the sensation of wonder; these things are at the very heart of archaeology. Archaeology is the opportunity to stand up to your knees in mud in pouring rain and still have the child-like amazement at everything the earth wants to give up.

With walking, the landscape is ever changing, not just because of passing through it, but because it will have changed the moment it has been walked through. Imperceptibly perhaps, but it will have changed: millions upon millions of tiny actions eroding or constructing the scene, with mankind constantly, sometimes casually, making an indelible mark. Archaeologists like tracing those marks, those footsteps, those echoes of humankind, wondering and recording their passing.

Wanting to know what yesterday was like is at the heart of archaeology. And the glorious thing about archaeology is the fact it's not all digging holes; there are myriad ways in which anybody can get involved.

So how to get involved where you live? For a starters join the Council for British Archaeology.

Every part of Britain has some story to tell which is woven into our soils, landscapes and buildings. This historic environment is one of our richest resources and gives a special quality to our lives. It is also irreplaceable. Yet, because we all live and work in it, it is easily overlooked or squandered. Nothing stays the same. Change made the past, just as it will shape the future. But we owe it to those who follow us to find ways of managing change so that they will have a past for themselves. This is why the CBA exists: to give a voice to Britain's past, and to help enrich the time to come.

The CBA is a network of individuals, national and regional organizations, and welcomes everyone with a concern for our historic environment. By joining you:

- Give us resources to develop our work in education, conservation and providing information.
- Strengthen the profile of archaeology in the minds of decision-makers.

Individual membership also brings:

- Six issues of our flagship magazine *British Archaeology*, including CBA briefings with projects and events in which you can get involved.
- Three issues of the members' newsletter, with news of the latest CBA projects and initiatives.
- Membership of a CBA region.
- A voice in the work of the Council.
- Our annual report.

Find out more at www.britarch.ac.uk

Council for British Archaeology
St Mary's House
66 Bootham
York YO30 7BZ
Tel: (+44) (0) 1904 671417
Fax: (+44) (0) 1904 67138

Email: info@britarch.ac.uk

KIT AND THE BASICS

'WALKING IN THE ROMAN ARMY'S FOOTSTEPS'

This is not an exhaustive list; the walker will have their own idea of what is needed, it is merely an aide memoire. The author cautions all walkers that there are extremes on this route which at any time of year may well catch out the unprepared. With an allocated time of ten days and a distance of

5 Told you it was a bit steep! On the way to Birdoswald

approximately 192km (give or take a stagger to a place of refreshment here or there), it is unlikely it will be heavenly blue skies all the way. The author cautions the walker to be suitably equipped and sensible to the conditions throughout.

Remember: If in doubt head for a place of warmth and comfort where ale is available.

Good Worn-in Boots

To enjoy a good walk, have the right boots; this is a reasonably tough expedition taking approximately nine or ten days if you are going to do it in one go, maybe longer if you are enjoying it enough. Here are some tips:

- A comfortable pair of walking boots is essential to tackle mud and a good few gallons of water.
- Plus, a pair of soft boots or shoes for town walking – there are three days of pavements and tarmac. It will be hard on the feet if you don't!
- Be properly prepared, wear-in new boots by wearing them to the office for a few weeks – you could start a trend!
- A well-ventilated foot is the thing. The Roman *caligae*, a flimsy-looking leather sandal, was designed to allow good airflow, cutting down on the chance for blisters to develop. Add studs and you can tramp over anything – and they did.
- Good sock will come in very useful – bring plenty!
- Carry a small towel at the top of your bag – it will come in very useful.

Waterproofs: An Essential

Cumbria and Northumberland are known for their own very special brands of liquid sunshine. A good-quality set of lightweight waterproofs, including over-trousers, is a must. Depending on the weather, 'full kit' is not required for Tynemouth and Newcastle. The first two days are city walking and lightweight tops are the order of the day. Rucksacks can be a problem in some locations in the city – stay light but do watch your personal effects, keep them close and safe.

A handy towel packed for immediate use, next to the dry socks, is likewise a must-have.

EXTREME CONDITIONS
Even in summer the exposed sections of this walk can be subject to severe weather. Wherever possible take shelter, preferably in a place which serves ale, and wait for the blast to pass. This can be difficult in some situations so the walker can experience exactly what it was like to be walking the Wall on a daily basis as a soldier. Remember, every experience along the way is part of the adventure – you never know where it will take you.

A DIVERSION CAUSED BY WEATHER IS TO BE ENJOYED
Take your time and allow longer than you think; have a plan 'Z'.
   The author will not be upset if you take the bus; indeed such initiative is essential on certain days. It allows the walker to enjoy not just the Wall, but the wider sense of place. The wall is not a hermetically sealed box, it is part of a living environment and should be seen as such.

DON'T FORGET THE MIDGE SPRAY!
No Roman equivalent other than twenty-year old fish sauce on the breath!

Bait: An Army Marches on its Stomach

This walk starts in Newcastle, no shortage of shops for provisioning at the eastern end; less so, beyond Corbridge. There are pubs along the way, but not all are open all day and some don't do food. Beyond Carlisle things get a tad thin on the provisions front. So be prepared.

Torch

A good torch is useless without batteries, so remember these. Alternatively, get a wind-up torch.

Plasters

Check for allergic reaction in advance.

Foot Plasters

Try them out before you need them.

Spare Insoles

An absolute must for some from the start; others may well need them towards the end of the walk.

Waterproof Container

It will rain or you will fall in a stream somewhere. It will happen. Protect your camera, GPS, iPod, etc. Also pack a map cover, for keeping bits and bobs close at hand, notepad (essential) along with a pencil or two, because pencils don't run in the wet. Clay pencils are ideal.

Space Blanket

An emergency thermal cover is extremely useful; it will stave off hyperthermia. It also comes in useful to sit on and takes up very little space. However, the author has never managed to get one back into its original bag. It will also act as an additional waterproof layer for your backpack in extremely rough conditions.

Whistle

Attach this to your outer clothing; make it easy to reach. The author knows from personal experience that this can be a lifesaver.

Hi-visibility Band

Useful, if not essential, especially if the walker is heading down from the Wall via the country roads at dusk. 'Be seen, be safe' is a wise motto – there are no street lights.

Observe & Record

You will see something new, because that is the way of things; the author has walked past many a feature sometimes for years without ever noticing what is under his nose. All it takes, in some instances, is the time of day, the angle of the sun and being in the right place (and that will vary by the moment).

The idea of this guide is for the walker to explore and not be fooled by us so-called specialists and experts. Anyone can experience the joy of discovery, but the real joy is making sure others can enjoy it too.

Take a photo, make a note and let English Heritage and the author know as soon as practicable.

 DO NOT attempt to excavate items, simply record and report.

Contacts

Covering: Cumbria

English Heritage
3rd floor Canada House
3 Chepstow Street
Manchester M1 5FW
Tel: 0161 242 1400
Fax: 0161 242 1401
Email: northwest@english-heritage.org.uk

Covering: Northumberland, Tyne and Wear

English Heritage
Bessie Surtees House
41–44 Sandhill
Newcastle-upon-Tyne NE1 3JF
Tel: 0191 269 1200
Fax: 0191 261 1130
Email: northeast@english-heritage.org.uk

The Author
Clifford Jones
Email: 1959cliffordjones@gmail.com

Where possible provide details of location, including a grid reference.

Provide: grid reference, latitude, longitude; eastings and northings – the skill of map reading is part of understanding the landscape you will be walking through, so learn as much as you can about how to do it properly. It could also save you time and effort and, in extreme cases, somebody's life. Alternatively use your GPS, but please make sure that it is correctly calibrated. A sketch is always useful: use any general features and then any local feature to assist the archaeologist standing in the middle of nowhere trying their very best to check on your findings.

Every bit of information helps put the archaeological picture together. The Wall is a big environment: the vallum wanders off away on its own; there are numerous Roman camps and native settlements. There is a lot to take in and knowing how to find what you're looking for is a blend of understanding a map and how to translate that information to the actual.

Observation is everything, as you go along the way it will come to you; it will creep up quite unexpectedly. Features will come to you and the ways of knowing how to interpret them with it. Whilst this can be taught in a classroom the only real way is to be out in the landscape and to learn hands-on.

> He sought to make himself acquainted with the province and known to the army …
>
> Tacitus, Agricola, trans. A.J. Church & W.J. Brodribb (London: Macmillan, 1877)

Common Sense

This is an invaluable resource. It comes free of charge and needs feeding with plenty of fresh air and time. No point in rushing; think things through. If the going is tough one day, break off and rest; this is no race. There are solutions to most of the needs to advance so many kilometres per day – only in the winter months is it difficult to find an alternative means of getting to certain locations.

Please keep to paths and help to keep erosion down; remember that agriculture plays an enormous part in the Northumbrian and Cumbrian economies, so close gates after you.

NOTICE REGARDING HERITAGE SITE OPENING TIMES

At the time of publication English Heritage have announced that due to the state of their finances relating to a massive cut in their budget (caused by an on-going national decline), some properties (Housesteads and Corbridge) along the Wall will be closed to the public in the winter months – October to March.

This does not affect access to the National Trail.

At the time of writing there is debate within Whitehall that English Heritage will be converted into a standalone body, as part of the government's move of certain parts of the nation's assets out of state control (sometimes referred to as the third estate). Hadrian's Wall is already someway there with its limited company status. As the present funding is being cut, can the situation get better in a completely standalone form?

This is not to be confused with the equally interesting decision regarding the transfer of publicly owned assets to voluntary community-run organisations: www.english-heritage.org.uk/publications/pillars-of-the-community-the-transfer-of-local-Authority-heritage-assets/pillars-of-the-community-the-transfer-of-local-Authority-heritage-assets/.

The author trusts the walker will do their own research and ask some pertinent questions, thus making their minds up and speaking out accordingly.

If the dog is brought along for the fun, make sure they keep the walker on a lead.

Definitely plan ahead, ring establishments (email in this instance doesn't have the opportunity for personal contact) to check opening times, they will vary with the seasons. If booking accommodation make sure the establishment knows where you are starting from to reach them; the locals know not only the distances, but the terrains. Overambitious agendas usually end in disaster; take local advice as this walk will take longer than you think. Talk to the locals along the way, gather information; use it as you need. In the summer there is quite a good National Trail bush telegraph as to conditions and places to stop. There is a genuine feeling of community along the Wall, add to it.

6 Norman walls on Roman foundations, Newcastle

GETTING THERE: RAIL IS BEST!

This walk starts in Tynemouth, easily reached from Newcastle by Metro. Newcastle is a fantastic spot for rail connections from all over the UK. Book your ticket well in advance to get some great deals. The author recommends to anyone that does not often travel by train that they should allow more time for connections than they think; most rail company search engines allow for this. The walk starts at Newcastle (from an arrival point of view) and ends at Kirkbride, with the nearest station at Wigton, on the Whitehaven to Carlisle line. The walker should head to Carlisle and then across to Newcastle for the return; this single ticket is available from the conductor as both services are currently run by the same company, Northern Rail.

The walker will have their fill of the infernal combustion engine throughout the walk, especially in Newcastle and Carlisle. The worst spots where the walker and car come into conflict are, in fact, in the countryside, not the town, where the pedestrian is given some basic facilities if not respect. Rail and public transport are undoubtedly the way ahead – after walking of course!

A Sort of Map

A compass comes in jolly useful, especially if wandering around north of the Wall. If not a compass, knowing how to use a GPS properly helps – buying one does not make the user an expert. A compass does not need batteries.

This guide does include very simple maps, whose lack of detail is deliberate: this is your adventure, all the author will do is point you in the right direction and coax you along it. The author's policy is to make sure the walker gets lost. That is most definitely part of the plan – remember this. If you want to understand the Wall it is essential not to have the author holding the walker's hand.

As the walk progresses the landscape will provide clues. What lies off this line? What's that over there? What's that bump?

That's where the adventure begins …

TRANSPORTS OF DELIGHT

NEXUS
www.nexus.org.uk/travel-information/journey-planner

Travel in and around Newcastle, and as far as Hexham, is part of NEXUS: this includes metro, rail and buses. The Metro service is excellent and frequent; however, if considering enjoying the odd ale, be aware there are no toilets at Metro stations. Primarily this is a ticket machine environment, so have some change handy; being caught without a ticket will hurt your pocket!

Buses are frequent on central and suburban routes, and cover reasonably long distances. However, Newcastle and environs are not an integrated system, so your ticket might well be only applicable to one particular service provider.

NEXUS owns the Metro system. DB Regio operates it in a typical efficient German manner. The Metro is undergoing a much-needed modernisation process; on Sundays the system is occasionally liable to partial closure; buses operate between stations instead.

7 The Victorian swing bridge atop the Roman river-crossing at Newcastle

▌Traveline North-east & Cumbria Journey Planner
http://jplanner.travelinenortheast.info

The Journey Planner is a fantastic travel information provider which you can access via your PDA (or just ring). Be precise in what you require; give it a try before you need it in earnest.

The only problem the author has identified in using the Journey Planner is knowing exactly where to type in the necessary information. As long as the walker has sight of a public building or street name, all is usually well.

Hadrian's Wall Bus AD122: Listed on NEXUS & Journey Planner
At the time of writing the Hadrian's Wall Bus AD122 service provides an excellent means of crossing the frontier. From the author's experience, those not used to public transport need a little assistance in using buses.

Newcastle Central Station is a busy spot and the AD122 bus stop is not obvious when you come through the barriers and out of the main entrance, so give yourself plenty of time. This goes for everywhere else that it stops and picks up from. The buses don't always stop automatically, so make it obvious you want to catch the bus. AD122 buses have a very obvious Hadrian livery; however, from time to time the service provider will use an ordinary bus. So if a bus turns up at the right time and it indicates 122, it's the bus!

QuayLink: Listed on NEXUS & Journey Planner
There is a brilliant service between The Baltic Centre for Community Art and The Sage art centre in Gateshead and Newcastle, and it is most definitely the best way to get up the very steep part of Grey Street – a fast and frequent service. The bus stops have digital displays showing bus times and services. Two routes are available, one to Haymarket and the other to Central Station.

Northumberland & Cumbria County Council subsidised bus routes
At the time of writing many of the services that have provided useful additional connections to spots along the way are under threat due to government cut backs.

Be sure that the timetable you're using is up to date. Check with Journey Planner North-east & Cumbria or Transport Direct to make sure.

ARRIVING

- **www.nationalrail.co.uk**

Newcastle Central Station is a magnificent structure. Opened in 1850, it set the standard for others to follow. Its frontage is kept in character with the rest of the city, which was busy being refashioned by the local architect John Dobson and builder Richard Grainger.

It is light and airy, especially on the exposed platform for Hexham and Carlisle! Indeed, in the case of the Carlisle platform (and often the stock used on the service) it seems as if it is an afterthought – more on this anon.

Having traversed the ridiculous, dangerous and unnecessary platform barriers erected in a futile attempt to protect private railway company profits, the walker has arrived in Newcastle

There are left-luggage facilities at this station, follow the signs.

The walker will have thundered up the East Coast mainline. If the train has decided (because of its age and the number of changes of livery weighing heavy on its bodywork) to break down, or is wistfully dawdling along because a leaf has, out of spite, placed itself for disposal on the line, then whichever, the walker will have become aware of distance; usually because of the time passed, rather than the land covered. Especially if there is an infant making everyone aware that teething is an unpleasant process, and a fellow passenger making it known that he is 'on the train' and 'very important' by yelling into a telephone every five minutes whilst tapping his notebook with the rapidity of a machine gun.

8 The adventure starts here!

The panoramic landscape sweeps by, the wonderful views blur with the odd great minster and Victorian station to interrupt the visage. The cocoon of the train puts a distance between the traveller and the histories outside. But look for the chap walking the old dog, or the lone cyclist making their way along some forgotten lane. They are useful characters; you can create stories from these anonymous spectres: what worlds they inhabit; where they are going to or coming from; what loves, lies and hopes dwell within? It will assist the elements around the walker in fading into the background.

Importantly, these visages outside, be they man on a bicycle or solitary passenger on a platform, they all fix the place. They are in it, you are passing through, yet you can imagine: take the path with them or turn the other way. You see them for a brief second, yet they can stay with you for a lifetime, because of where they were. The light, shade, circumstance, the walker's emotion and empathy, all play their part in building a picture framed by space.

The walker can stare at the same stones as the builders of the Wall; yet, does the walker see what the builders saw? Search for clues, establish a position, consider the factors, look at the mistakes, theorise. The ability is to build a picture with many pieces missing, yet one in which there is enough left to provide a framework for the landscape and the Wall to hang within. All the emotions are required, otherwise the walker will just see stones and that is not the purpose of the adventure.

The author remembers looking from the dining car window of the Paris to Madrid night train, out into the fields of France on a warm summer's evening, the seas of corn and sunflowers, and one man on a bicycle, breaking the silence a solitary note in a symphony of space. It was the man on the bicycle that made the scenery come alive, gave it scale, stature, grandeur, and primarily a history. It reminded the author that understanding the past and present is a balance of scale, and how very little we actually know without an anticipation of the presence of man. Humankind passes, leaves a track and it is history.

From the carriage window the author realised he was cocooned, a mere observer with a momentary glimpse into a landscape that changed every second. The man on the bicycle proved a flash of reality; a bridge between the observer and the observed linked via the landscape. For that one brief moment the author could connect with that place and time; take in the landscape with new eyes as he could visualize it through the man on the bicycle. A momentary realisation that perception of history is just that, a mere perception; at best a blurred echo of the actual, unless there is something that stands out and, in the author's case, it was the man and the bicycle. The author could experience the person within it, giving scale, depth, life and a path for the history of the place to pass along.

How we look at history depends on where we stand. He was passing through the history of the man on the bicycle, an observer; the cyclist was passing through his – paths crossed. The author on a predetermined speedy path, the cyclist at ease to do as he pleased, dependant only on the turn of a pedal, fast or slow; reason for travel unknown. Desire and destination? Beyond the author's understanding; but the cyclist was there creating a part of history.

The author's life was on a course, led by rails; the cyclist was free to turn the wheel, stop, stare and go another way. The author's view of the scene was fixed; the cyclist's variable.

The walker should look at the Wall not just as a physical structure, but as a tangible link between our perceptions and those of the builders and users; consider them, as much as the stone.

Now take a moment to transform the man with the old dog, plodding along the track, into two soldiers walking the military way with easy gait. No hurry for them, away from duty on the Wall, heading for the nearest bar in the village just over the hill; one is complaining to the other that his belt clip is broken and he has lost the metal stud from it. The man on the bicycle becomes a cavalry officer organising the gathering of fodder for the winter, his horse is annoyed by the flies. The officer calms him as he is trying to write a note to his lover; he curses as he drops the stylus to the ground. The horse then stands on it.

We glimpse the past for a second and it is gone, but at least we have the ability to see a trace of it again. The stud and the stylus connect us all to a moment and a place.

Without the human trundling by in his or her own moment of history, the scale of all landscape is meaningless; there is not a spot along the route of this adventure that man has not altered, destroyed, rebuilt, farmed, quarried, mined or left as lost. These are not random acts; they follow upon actions and consequences. The walker needs to consider the sequences of these processes. The landscape and environment is the clue; impose an external action, an imposition to build a structure and the results are all around.

The Wall is more than an ancient, half-hidden monument packaged as a tourist attraction, it is a space inhabited by humankind; some you can talk to, some you can only hope to hear via a whisper on the wind. Yet you will hear all with clarity if you take the time to listen, and will see if you just look and look again; you will see. It's up to you. Let the landscape in: the roll of the hills, the Whin Sill, the Carlisle Plain, the farmsteads, the great cattle enclosures, the forts and camps.

How the walker interprets the Wall experience is up to the walker; it is a wholly personal thing. There will be moments when the walker wonders what they are doing on a bleak bit of Whin Sill when the sun turns to rain and the wind takes the easy route straight through their trousers. But the author suggests that once the walker has spent a day or so out in the wider landscape and is 'into' the walk, the past will become apparent. The rain and the wind are eternal, along with the sunsets; it all comes together rather well. Sweat is still sweat and a thirst still needs to be quenched and the day's experience is to be savoured; the effort is worth it.

The walker is the adventurer and all the author is doing is providing a strand to hold on to as you discover your own man with the old dog, or solitary cyclist.

Exploratio

Exploratio is the Roman name for a military scouting party: a small group or sometimes an individual scout whose job is to evaluate the terrain around, learning of what, where and when, developing potential scenarios and strategies, working a path through the hostile landscape. Most importantly, they would identify safe pathways (with a few held in reserve should circumstances change), and operate with an ability to look at all aspects without blinkers.

If the walker arrived from Carlisle on the Newcastle and Carlisle railway, you will have travelled on an early railway of great importance, connecting the east and west coasts in 1838, following to some degree the intended canal first promoted in 1794. Such was the desire to connect the two points and allow for faster traffic across the country and ultimately the Atlantic.

From Carlisle you will have had a leisurely journey with a preview of what you are about to take on, though most of the useful stations are long closed.

Notice the contrast between the two city stations. Carlisle station is a sorry sight in comparison with Newcastle; there is little bustle and urgency about the place, which goes deeper than just the state of the railway stations and services. It is a dark reflection of a wide divide in fortunes, investment and confidence. The lack of facilities and infrastructure within Cumbria is the key reason for starting this journey in the east. A sad but realistic indictment of the state of the county is its desire to rely solely upon tourism in its central belt and the stub end of nuclear power to the west.

9 Echoes of another imperial age?

GET TO KNOW YOUR WALL

Understanding the Wall in detail is a challenge; the various features and how they are supposed to work keeps academics busy writing volumes and reports that nobody other than fellow academics will ever see. A general public view has been agreed, adopted and used on Wall interpretation boards – for the most part very well. It would be remiss of the author not to identify the various parts, but unlike others he will give no specific answer to their actual purposes, in particular of one of the major features, the vallum, as there is no definitive answer. The rest: the Wall acted as a block; advanced ditch, a means of slowing down a charging force; turrets, milecastles and forts support the control and administration of the Wall.

The English Heritage cross-section assists, found at: www.english-heritage. org.uk/professional/research/landscapes-and-areas/national-mapping-programme/hadrians-wall-nmp/hadrians-wall-construction-of-wall/.

A Wall is just that, it keeps things in or keeps things out; how effectively it does it is dependent upon many factors. However, in this case the Wall does not exist in isolation, it comes with added components. In advance of the Wall facing north, for this is one thing we can be certain of, the Wall is for looking at the north in detail. There lies a ditch, sometimes described as the north ditch, which in Latin is a *fossa*; in this there could be some unpleasant thorn bushes hiding sharpened stakes to discourage the odd blackberry picker. The sloping edge towards the Wall glacis reveals the enemy for a long enough time to allow them to be shot down, followed by a small berm, flat ground immediately underneath the Wall. The Wall, which is probably 6m high with regular stone protective shields for defenders, turrets and milecastles incorporated into it, is of stone, replacing an original turf and palisade structure (western side only). Behind the Wall is a supply road or in some places pack-horse way due to the terrain. Then there is a vallum (or valla), a 6m-wide, 3m-deep ditch, the purpose of which is utterly unclear – at best a third line of defence if the Wall is considered a defendable barrier. This vallum is, at places, immediately behind the Wall, or, at others, some considerable distance away (up to 700m). Construction of all features of the Wall show variation due to the different builders used at different times in the Wall's history.

Further information on valla can be found here: www.dur.ac.uk/resources/ archaeological.services/research_training/hadrianswall_research_framework/ project_documents/Vallum.pdf.

The author hopes that the walker will develop a theory, especially regarding the vallum – as 'we' have no idea as to its purpose, the walker is as justified in an opinion as any of us. As the author has stood in it, scrambled on his hands and knees in it, fallen into it, been up to his thighs in mud in it (assisted by a curious herd of cows eager to add their opinion), he is willing to take on any new ideas.

As for milecastles, they do vary a bit along the way; not unexpected considering the different builders involved in the job. Milecastles appear every mile (no surprise there), except this is a Roman mile, that is 1,479m or 1000 paces, *mille passuum*. There are around 80 milecastles; there may have been more, and some have completely vanished because of Roman refurbishment and rebuilding. From an archaeological perspective there are inscriptions which aid identification for three distinctive designs, all of which roughly match a square design of 18m x 15m and 21m x 18m for the turf ones on the western frontier. Each milecastle had a turret to match the other three divided out equally along the Roman mile, providing a regular look-out system over the entire wall. Examples of legionary variation of design have been identified at: milecastle 9 Chapel House, which is an easily recognised long-axis milecastle, likely to be the work of Legio VI Victrix; milecastle 37 Housesteads West, which is squat, short axis and the work of the most notable Legio II Augusta; and the 'King's Stable' at Poltross Burn, Gilsland Legio Valreia Victrix, which has a double barrack block. Turrets also show variation and there is at least one signal tower incorporated into the Wall. All will be revealed, or as much as possible based on research to date, as the walker makes their way along.

The walker must remember the numbering system is pure fantasy.

Do take time to look at the remains that are presented; they are not merely stones on stone. Consider how they were lived in. Think about a wet night in February: how much warmth and comfort could you get out of such a building? What effect would the place have on morale? Would fellowship of your colleagues rank high? What was the system of patrolling management? Where did clothes dry out? Where was the latrine? How long does it take to get from the milecastle to the first turret in the dark? How comfortable was the arrangement in these lonely but regular sentinels?

Use these questions along the way, adapt to the structure and think up more. They all add to the walker's picture of the circumstance, the landscape and the Wall within it. How and why should be at the front of the mind; the Wall cannot be taken for granted, even when it is absent.

It is time to get started; time to get marching along with the wind in the face, with a good dollop of sunshine on the head and the best of Northumberland and Cumbrian scenery for the eye. The author can guarantee the walker will be busy for a couple of weeks and will finish this walk with a different perspective of the Wall than when they started.

GET TO KNOW YOUR TYPICAL ROMAN FORT

Principia (Headquarters Building)

The *principia* was generally divided into three main sections: a courtyard with verandas on three sides; a basilica, consisting of a nave and one aisle, for instruction and meetings of officers; and lastly a range of rooms for senior fort administrators, with their piles of daily orders to be duly assigned, working in rooms at the rear of the building. It is often considered that the fort garrison could assemble at the *principia*, but the practicalities of space suggest that this would be for officers who would then pass on the instructions and news accordingly. The basilica would probably have clerestory windows high in the walls to allow as much light as possible into the space. There would be a raised platform (tribunal) allowing the commanding officer to stand a head above the officers and to get his voice to the back of the room without having to strain when issuing instructions. The rear of the structure was for the shrine (*Aedes*), which would include the legions' standards, and other military and religious paraphernalia. There were separate rooms associated with the shrine, but with very practical purposes of management of the fort and the protection of imperial funds, normally held in a vault beneath the shrine itself in a strong room. There was an office for the fort adjutant (*Cornicularius*) and another for the standard bearers (*Signiferi*), whose major task was as pay officer. There was good sense in putting both these officers within the influence and safety of the shrine: the gods could be seen in assisting in their duties by offering protection, although the pay clerk tended to have the additional safety of grills across the windows, just in case the gods took a day off and somebody decided to give themselves a substantial pay rise.

Praetorium (Commandant's House)

Officers in the Roman army tended to come from the middle to elite classes, so a certain standard was expected. As such, a typical atrium house was the norm, which, because of the origins of such a structure being in the sunny Mediterranean, didn't really suit the far north of Britain. Based around an open courtyard, they would have not been particularly pleasant spots and much alteration is recorded along the Wall. Hypocausts were fitted (heating being an absolute essential) as were private bathhouses, to allow for some privacy – especially to discuss the latest news from Rome and promotions in the legion. Bathhouses were as much about socialising and communication as they were getting clean – though they did also come in useful for thawing out after a cold day on the Wall. There would be a reception room for entertaining, a dining room and bedrooms, including accommodation for official guests, and, tucked out of the way at the back of the building, were the kitchen and services. The author considers that many commanders' wives only used the *praetorium* for official events and in many cases lived out in the *vicus* (settlement outside of the fort), where there seems to have been better accommodation, designed to better cope with the weather.

Horrea (Granaries)

Granaries are often the last buildings to vanish on a Roman site; they were very well built and stood on raised platforms to keep their contents dry and ventilated. Exactly how they were laid out is unclear, but they stood tall, with buttresses and an internal wooden floor, often offering more than one storey for storage. They held not only grain, but also imported products, no doubt including oils. They would have posed a major fire risk and there is evidence that they required major maintenace and rebuilding on a regular basis.

Barracks

There is really no typical Roman barrack block. Occasionally in groups of ten, sometimes considered to be an echo of the troops in the field, with a communal cooking facility, the practicalities of Roman forts see the barracks rebuilt, reorganised and rebuilt again on a regular basis. There were general features, verandas, which were absolutely essential given the weather, and possibly external wooden screens providing windbreaks. The more sophisticated barrack blocks were built of stone, though some were never completed in stone throughout. Use of these barracks is not as straightforward as may appear.

Some barracks were converted to stables, though some stables were purpose built, depending on the legion. However, the idea of a large number of horses inside a fort is just not practical. This leads the author to his favourite subject: who actually lived in a fort? More on this anon.

Valetudinarium (Hospital)

Apart from the facility at Housesteads, which includes a small plunge bath, no other Wall hospital has been identified. Every fort had one, but the office, like many others required to make the machinery of the army work, is still not understood.

With an understanding of the principal buildings, start to put the individuals, functions and interactions into place. Sometimes the walker may notice potential clashes, occasionally because of the need to portray a specific period in the restoration, but there will be times when there really are still some unanswered queries, especially regarding barracks and the operation of some forts. The walker should look at the basics: water and sewage systems; location in the landscape; what can and cannot be seen.

GETTING STARTED

- **Soft shoes needed**
- **NEXUS Metro map – available from Newcastle TIC**

This is down to the individual's own initial travel arrangements, but think and plan ahead before you begin, then throw your plans away and have another go. Time spent on this will pay dividends later.

Always allow more time than you expect to need – the author cannot emphasise this point enough. Distance is not the only factor to consider: terrain, actual path conditions, features and anomalies you may discover will slow things down. It is the hidden things that tend to take time – worth attention, but try to keep to a timetable. Mud and weather slows the body down and the exposed nature of much of the route can play tricks on the walker. If walking as a party, always allow for the slowest person. This may not become apparent until the end of the third day, but the author has allowed for a warming-up period and knows that getting the pace right is difficult. All parties should remember that the Wall is the focus, not the speed of progress; thus the slowest member may assist the group by allowing everyone the time to observe.

This walk takes a good ten days, because two days should be spent in and around Tynemouth and Newcastle: there is plenty to see and do, and there is plenty to learn before getting under way. Why rush? If the walker wishes to shorten the experience or do it in parts, so be it. Always start the day with the same principle: It is not the distance that matters, it is the experience, knowledge and understanding. The author wishes the walker to gain enough experience, and detail and sense of place, to ask questions of him and others.

The author knows of people that have run the Wall in less than 24 hours. It can be done by running through the night – though it is hard to understand how much enjoyment can be had, other than in a sense of personal achievement, by doing this. The author has seen the state of the runners afterwards.

In Roman times a restricted military document could be sent with one rider and a great number of horse changes from one end of the Wall to the other in a day. Not a comfortable experience for the rider. Numerous theories relating to signalling along the Wall have been suggested. There certainly are signal stations, mostly for outlying forts, the operation of which would have been very variable, especially in winter.

Even if very fit and able to march along the route, don't; the result will be the missing of so much. The author is not fit, he never has been, he enjoys his beer and food too much, yet he has managed the Wall for years. Observation is the thing, taking one's time, stopping, taking the air. This goes for the city as well as the countryside. The dip of a pavement, the slight drop of a building line: they are all possible clues.

There are great hotels and hostels in Newcastle and the author is not going to waste anyone's time telling them which to go for; you choose as you think fit. If you can get a view of the Tyne at a reasonable price and enjoy a lively night life go for it; you won't be disappointed. The author spent many happy years in Newcastle and still enjoys the city when he has the time.

Go to the Newcastle and Gateshead TIC website for all your hotel needs. It is run by very helpful people; nothing is too much trouble to get you started and experiencing Newcastle.

▌Newcastle and Gateshead TIC
www.newcastlegateshead.com/site/plan-your-visit/tourist-information

The people of Newcastle upon Tyne and environs are a friendly lot. The author arrived from his academic sojourn at Oxford many years ago and never regretted the move. He was already aware, having lived in Cumbria, that people in the north talked to each other; something that the southerners tend not to do. People in Newcastle are expressive and for the most part extremely caring individuals; they enjoy culture. The Laing Gallery, live music and theatre all thrive here; not simply because a city has to have these things, but because the people are not frightened to be vocal, take part and believe in themselves. They are strong through effort and a determination not to be stood upon by circumstance; they deliver as good as they get; they are determined and rise above the ordinary every day. If there is a football match on and the walker has the time, get a ticket, even if you have no great interest in football; the author believes it is the closest anyone can get to being in the Colosseum for sound and atmosphere – truly amazing. On a Saturday the roar can be heard for miles and echoes deep into the city's ancient stonework, it is welcomed, gathered up, gently stored away as memories of a great and noble place.

Newcastle United Football Club
www.nufc.co.uk

Most of the present city is to the area north of the Wall. The walker will realise that the city slopes down towards the Wall; it does not take the high ground. Newcastle Roman Fort (or Pons Aelius) is the original terminus, but it is a very exposed one. There is a great deal more to be understood about Roman Newcastle.

OFF YOU GO

- **Have some change ready**
- **Best time of day to start is 9.45 a.m. to get the most out of the attractions and sites**
- **Note: No toilets on Metro trains or stations**

Start at Newcastle station at the Metro, clearly signposted with a big 'M'.

Head down the steps to the ticket machines and buy a Metro Day Saver (after 9 a.m.) All Zone ticket. This allows you unlimited travel on the Metro and ferry, so it gives the chance for some exploring off route, which is what this is all about.

The signs and system is very similar to any metro anywhere in the world, so follow the signs for Monument and then Tynemouth, and look for the destination indicator for the train you need. Don't worry if you miss one, there will be another along in a few minutes or so; the Metro is a fast and frequent system. You will have to change at Monument, depending on the service. This isn't a great problem and is easy to follow, normally from Platform 2 to Platform 3 at Monument. Look and listen for the announcement. The indicators are very easy to follow, plus the locals are very helpful.

Metro trains are built for short-distance commuting with plenty of standing room; there is always bunching around the doors at peak times, but off peak there is usually a seat to be found and the best ones are looking out of the front window. A driver's eye view of the track from Monument to Tynemouth – smashing!

The journey takes about 39 minutes, so there is plenty to see along the way.

START Central Station–Monument–Manors–Byker–Chillingham Road–Walkergate–Wallsend–Hadrian Road–Howdon–Percy Main–Meadow Well–North Shields–Tynemouth **END**

The view offers a great variety of insights. For an industrial view, note the Byker Bridge, built in 1878 over the Ouseburn. The Ouseburn is worth a diversion and if you plan your trip well you may enter a forgotten tunnel under Newcastle: the Victoria Tunnel. A very special experience indeed; don't miss it.

▌The Victoria Tunnel
www.ouseburntrust.org.uk

Further along the line you pass through Wallsend. You will be back here later.

The view here could be described as uninspiring – post-industrial – in fact it is a reviving industrial area, with the Tyne re-emerging as a base for the deep-sea oil industry and wind turbine generators. New business parks have replaced collieries. Massive government investment has taken time to show results, but it has blossomed. There is a dramatic contrast between the stainless steel, concrete and glass edifices and the snaggle-toothed rows of nineteenth-century housing, the colliery villages and the Byker Wall. However, both views are equal in importance in understanding our past and present.

Percy Main takes its name from the community around Percy Main, Howden Panns colliery. The Durham Mining Museum offers an insight to this site and many others.

▌Durham Mining Musem
www.dmm.org.uk

Not far to go and Tynemouth is reached. For those not wanting to see Tynemouth, alight at North Shields and head directly to the well-signposted (if gloomy-entranced) ferry jetty.

This grand station of 1882 was built by the North Eastern Railway. The North Eastern saw the possibilities for Tynemouth: commuter traffic, which explains the old bay platforms, and day trippers to the coast. The Metro has brought new life to this station and, whilst it no longer has quite the day-to-day bustle of its former glory, the space is well used, especially at weekends. The author remembers spending many happy Sunday mornings at the market, which takes place on the concourse; since then, Saturday farmers' markets and Christmas markets have flourished. Please support this very popular community venue.

▌Tynemouth Market
www.tynemouth-market.com

Head out of the station and turn left, then at the junction turn right on to Manor Road, and then down to the crossroads onto the appropriately named Front Street – a wide expanse of comfortable-looking buildings portraying a rich and indulgent past. Turn right on to Pier Road and follow the signs for the castle, priory and battery.

▌Castle, Priory and Battery
www.english-heritage.org.uk/daysout/properties/tynemouth-priory-and-castle

As this English Heritage property is not open all year round, it would not be appropriate to make the start of the walk within the walls, but at the gatehouse instead. This impressive stone edifice was completely hidden until 1936, when the eighteenth-century office block built around it burned down. A castle has stood here since at least 1095 and a priory possibly even earlier.

Historically there has been bad blood between Newcastle and Tynemouth since public records began. The priory needed revenue and saw the obvious opportunities of being the first port of call for marine trade. The people of Newcastle saw it differently. The priory expansion provided a fish and salt business, but Newcastle got everything else.

As for Roman activity, this rocky spot at the mouth of the River Tyne would have seen some Roman structure, perhaps not a fort but a *pharos* (lighthouse), a beacon for shipping, which is an absolute necessity to avoid vessels coming to grief on the Black Middens, rocks lying just out of the estuary mouth. Indeed, the prospects for getting in and out of the Tyne were in the lap of the gods; with every tide the sand bars covering the rocks would move, making it an extremely perilous passage.

To negotiate this constantly changing estuary there were Roman naval forces based close at hand, to assist in checking the channel on a daily basis; these were based at Arbeia Roman fort, South Shields. At one time they were bargemen transferred from the River Tigris.

The author has always considered this exposed spot at Tynemouth priory to be just that, exposed and rocky. Any administration of shipping movements for the purposes of taxation cannot be done from a cliff top, but rather further back at a spot in line with Arbeia on the southern bank. More of that anon.

10 The Black Gate. A fortified gatehouse added to Newcastle Castle in the thirteenth century.

One thing that is very obvious: this peninsula has been a watch point for as long as humankind has walked the earth, longer than the North Sea has washed away at its base, back to a time when the Tyne met the Rhine. This cliff top would have stood out, a place of refuge above the treetops. When the waters had taken the land it would have been a site of refuge; the first point for any traveller, a beacon point and thus both of practical and spiritual importance long before Christianity gained its first foothold.

11 Welcome to Norman Newcastle – just a few steps

The neat, grassy slopes betray the previous hustle and bustle of the sites, all intermingled: priory, fort and battery. However, so much activity has ultimately diminished the chances of finding evidence of early humankind. The priory contains a reused statue base believed to come from Wallsend. Perhaps it did or perhaps, as the author suspects, it came from North Shields; time and research will tell.

It seems far too odd, when you stand on the peninsula, to consider that the most deliberate physical statement of Roman rule didn't smack you straight in the face as you approached Britannia, but waited for you to round the corner, as if hiding itself away – the terminus of Hadrian's Wall. Emperors are not noted for being shy – something is very wrong.

The Roman influence on Tynemouth is a mystery which needs further investigation. It seems impossible that the Romans had no effect on the area. Even if there was no formal frontier, the land mass would have seen farmsteads, settlements for fishing; yet the records are empty. Industrialisation from the eighteenth century onwards cannot account for the dearth of Roman material beyond Wallsend. The fact that Roman stones at the priory are thought to have been moved to the site suggests that there was an acceptance that there couldn't be anything Roman on the spot. Odd? Very.

THE WALK

DAY 1

TYNEMOUTH TO NEWCASTLE

THE WALK STARTS HERE

The walker has many miles and adventures to undertake, so before setting off, consider some refreshment before the ardours and adventures of the day. The author suggests, if the hour is right, The Priory on Front Street. There are other excellent outlets to try, so do feel free to sample a beverage and boost the local economy. Plenty of coffee shops and cafes are available for those taking it easy, and fish and chips are on offer if starting late in the morning. Those wishing to wander and look at the sea have plenty of opportunity. But do not linger long; there is walking to be done and questions to be answered.

Why has the author brought you to Tynemouth when the Wall finishes at Wallsend? Originally the Wall terminated at Newcastle with an extension being built to Wallsend; this extension was only one of a series of changes to the Wall after it was conceived.

As the author has already suggested, the earliest Roman frontier seems to have been merely a road with camps, forts, towers and ditches as required, temporary structures to assist further Roman advance.

The natural geology and geographic divide created by the path of the Tyne provides a clue to this frontier's situation. The rivers are ancient navigations and boundaries between tribes; they are known pathways. Where the river runs out, the east–west geological Whin Sill rift allows relatively easy passage through to the River Irthing, which is the key waterway towards Carlisle.

So the author starts the intrepid walker at Tynemouth?

On the Cumbrian coast, the terminus of the Wall frontier has a fort, a harbour, good communications and a frontier system. This is the difference between the two. So far we cannot find any Roman formality, any barrier or frontier defence, turret or vallum, to connect Wallsend to Tynemouth on the north side of the river. The coast doesn't portray itself in the way it does to the west. Whether the Wall was ever extended as an additional 'add on', like the stretch from Newcastle to Wallsend, is open to debate; no archaeological evidence has yet been discovered to settle the matter – but that does not mean none exists: 'absence of evidence is not evidence of absence'. From an archaeologist's point of view, the author would like a bit of digging to prove absolutely the absence, as he has his own theory!

This undoubted gap opens up a huge hole in the frontier debate that classical historians and archaeologists alike tend to brush over. So the author will ask the walker to pose the question 'what about those exposed few miles of wall absent, unprotected territory that would allow the natives unrestricted access to the southern shore of the Tyne?'

The walker can either join the theorists that consider that Arbeia, the Roman fort on the southern bank of the Tyne, adequately protected this area, or join those that adhere to the 'we haven't found the answer yet' theory.

The answer may lie in the fact that we put too much faith in a physical wall; that Roman military engagement with the landscape and people is more sophisticated and embroiled than we have previously imagined.

Certainly Trajan's fort works, occupying earlier works from Kirkbride and Bowness-on-Solway via Stanwix to the River Corbridge, offer a fluid means of defence or protection requiring cavalry to offer a rapid response, available at a moment's notice, with regular connecting patrols. No need to physically join the sites together in a constant chain. This policy applies to the area from Wallsend to Tynemouth, even after Hadrian had ordered a physical barrier. A perfectly reasonable option; yet not very grand and Hadrian liked the grand and physical.

The author is in the 'we haven't found the answer yet' camp; he cannot accept that an imperial order and prestigious military project fails to encompass the whole area. Indeed, the change in the original design, with the extension from Newcastle to Wallsend, makes one consider that somebody pointed out that the bridge across the Tyne some distance from the sea could hardly be called a complete cross-country barrier. It was a bit obvious when you sailed up the Tyne that something was missing if you looked north. This makes the author consider, based on the tribal archaeological settlement remains, that local political arrangements with the tribes may have played their part in the delay and lack of frontier for some time and, in the case of Tynemouth, its apparent complete absence.

The establishment of forts at Halton Chester, High Rochester, to Learchild (Votadinum) NU1011 could be the answer; they control a very large area of land and act as an extremely deep area of protection for the Tyne. This would be the pared back version of an earlier system, as mentioned earlier. There may well have been a diplomatic arrangement with the Selgovae with a partial partition of the territory to the east which started before Hadrian and was reduced from Halton Chesters to a new starting point at Newcastle, then reduced again during the building of the Wall to Wallsend. Perhaps part of the arrangement was that there was to be no physical wall preventing the Selgovae access to the north bank of the Tyne; in return for grain, workforce and general co-operation.

Forts along the Wall on the eastern side of the Pennines, in general, have more entrances on the north of the Wall. Perhaps this is another clue?

Archaeological research is the key; the forts and camps are there and many have never been formally excavated. But that is for another day.

You see! You are involved in archaeology and the walk hasn't even started yet. Theory is a major component, but it does need something to cling to in the way of facts. Theorising is best undertaken over a pint by a warming fire while letting aching limbs relax.

The walker needs to do just that: walk. Thus instructed, the walker should now proceed towards North Shields along the coastal walkway, which can be reached if the walker heads southwards; both routes meet water. All these various ways pass the imposing Admiral 'Father' Collingwood memorial, reminiscent of the fact that somewhere around here must be a large Roman temple to the gods for those either about to leave on or just returned from passage across the North Sea, with no doubt an image of Hadrian in union with the gods. Collingwood was genuinely respected by the ordinary sailors, hence 'Father'; the respect the Roman military held for Hadrian would be indicative of some affectionate term and statue – it does not survive.

The way westward to North Shields is easy, pleasant and bracing; depending on the tide it can be wet with spray. Along this stretch you will find the fish quay (you might smell it first); a great place to be at any time and an excellent venue for festivals. However, do take a moment to find a much hidden away archaeological gem: Clifford's Fort.

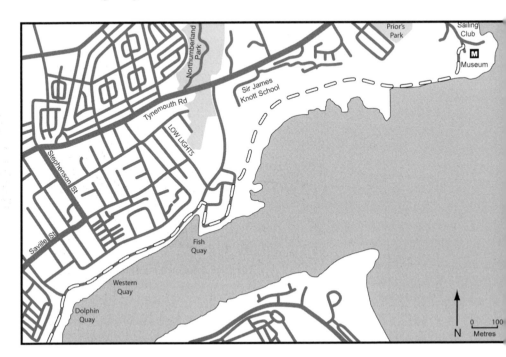

Clifford's Fort
http://sine.ncl.ac.uk/view_structure_information.asp?struct_id=1565

Somewhere along this stretch the author believes there was a very much earlier fort, a Roman one, specifically to pair with the fort on the opposite bank. Considering the difficult estuary mouth, there would be considerable traffic waiting for assistance out of the estuary; allowing for the type of craft, wind directions and the simple necessity to find shelter, the use of both sides of the estuary at this point seems an absolute necessity. The Romans liked administration, or to be precise taxation; one pays for the other and it was the military that made sure everybody complied. No tax money, no wages for the military; no military, no administration.

Boats all bobbing around in close contact with each other equals opportunity for tax avoidance and smuggling, rowdy sailors, the need for places of refreshment and other services.

Attempting to restrict this to one side of the river is not practical, so a location overseeing it all seems the best way to keep a stern and watchful eye.

12 It's not all Roman: the seventeenth-century Clifford's Fort, North Shields, revealed after centuries of obscurity. Definitely worth a look

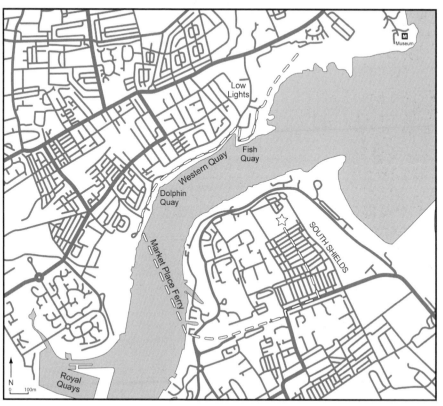

The author's best guess for the fort site based on his research is just above the fish quay. This would put it in a commanding position above the present fish quay. It would also offer a commanding view for a massive statue which would appear to a ship proceeding in on the tide to be standing in the middle of the river, and act as the mid-way marker between the *pharos* at Tynemouth and Arbeia fort.

Follow the signs for the ferry to South Shields; the river is a pleasant contrast to the gloomy approach, containing a bright, lightweight floating building which always amazes the author as to how well it withstands the blast of north-east weather.

Use your NEXUS ticket on the ferry. Enjoy the crossing, a mini-cruise and a wonderful way to experience the Tyne.

So far the walker will have been to Tynemouth only to be told that there probably was only a *pharos* and that there was no Wall, or at least none has been found; that there might just be a fort above the fish quay, but nobody has checked it out.

Perhaps not the brightest of starts but things are going to get better.

The walker should consider themself a trailblazer. When it comes to Wall walking the walker has gone further east than most and have the opportunity to get involved in archaeological theory and research.

We, the archaeologists and historians, certainly do not know everything; feel free to have a go.

On arrival at South Shields the walker has some options. At the main road either turn left along River Drive and its new housing, skirting the restored shipyard dry docks, or turn right into the town of South Shields.

DESTINATION: ARBEIA ROMAN FORT

- **www.twmuseums.org.uk/arbeia**

Using the quickest route: walk up to the main road, turn right at the roundabout, turn left along East Street to the far end and bear left and then right on to King Street; pass the Metro station; keep on going on to Ocean Road until you see a left turn marked 'Roman Road'. March down Roman Road. The fort is at the end. Turn left on to Fort Street and right on to Baring Street to get the full effect.

Now, that's better! Something physical, big, complete – well at least the gatehouse is: a full reconstruction and quite magnificent. At the rate they are going at Arbeia they will have the whole place rebuilt in another couple of years. Bit by bit it rises from the past.

Enjoy the visit, take your time, especially regarding the gatehouse; get the scale, the detail – you will not see the same again along the way. When faced by a windswept lump in the ground with a couple of sheep on top and you are told this was the gateway of a fort, you at least have something in mind for reference for future use.

Arbeia can only trace its archaeological roots to about AD 125; however, there are good reasons to consider that there is another earlier facility close by, possibly just to the south-west of the present fort platform. It would seem very unlikely that this location was left devoid of any Roman control before that date. If there was not, then there was no Roman control as far inland as Pons Aelius, which, considering the advanced state of Roman control of the north by the early 120s, doesn't make sense. The *vicus* lies beneath the present South

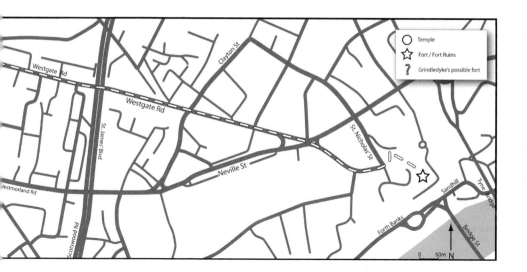

Shields that the walker has just walked through; it seems quite appropriate that the *vicus* and the town area are one and the fort is very much part of the community in which it sits.

Tyne & Wear Museum service and its dedicated, hard-working staff are doing a magnificent job in presenting the past. Excavations continue and further reconstruction of the fort provides the public with a better understanding of the Roman world. The author supports the desire of the museum in attempting to find a site for a new museum complex to house what has been

Above: 13 A gallery of arches at Arbeia Roman Fort, South Shields. Compare this to the church at Jarrow

Left: 14 A sturdy colonnade at Arbeia Roman Fort, South Shields

discovered thus far; it is hoped that a site can be found in the very near future. Like so many other archaeological sites, it is not the excavation that is the difficult part; the true time and costs come in the conservation, restoration, presentation and safe storage of artefacts. Please support this project by making a contribution; the author hopes you will agree it deserves support.

Having spent a good hour or more at Arbeia, the walker should now head back to the town centre and the Metro station.

DESTINATION: JARROW METRO STATION FOR BEDE'S WORLD

DAY 1

• **www.bedesworld.co.uk**

START South Shields–Chichester–Tyne Dock–Bede–Jarrow **END**
Catch the local bus service 526 or 527 (you will need to pay for this separately). This is a must of a visit.

Bede provides the most popular early history of the English-speaking people. The author would point out that the Welsh monk Gildas actually did a great deal of the background work with his *De Excidio Britanniae* (*On the Ruin of Britain*), but that does not take anything away from Bede and his effort.

Importantly, the walker will be seeing a post-Roman world or, to be precise, a world still influenced by Rome but in a very different way: by religion. The western Roman Empire collapsed in the fifth century, leaving the only remaining strand of a central control mechanism: Christianity, itself the product of a period when the powerful realised being pope was more influential than being emperor.

The first day has seen the walker visit Tynemouth, North and South Shields, and Jarrow. Not bad for day one.

Time for refreshment!

Take the bus back into Jarrow and take the Metro to Monument, or whichever stop is closest to your hotel.

Newcastle Nightlife

Newcastle has a fantastic nightlife, there is something for everyone. The author will not attempt to list it – just get out there and enjoy. You can dine well at little cost if you seek out the hidden places.

The author offers one favourite spot, which is not in the city centre, but out at Sandyford; take a taxi to Café Sapori on Starbeck Avenue. Simple, delicious rustic Italian cooking; food at its very best, served with devotion, a smile and not a little love. Take a bottle with you, but give them a ring first. A takeaway service is available.

There is one other establishment that must be visited; the finest of city pubs and spiritual home of the author. It is not easy to find, but that is half the fun and indeed a challenge. The author will be surprised if you find it at the first attempt.

The Crown Posada on Side

This is quite simply the most wonderful of pubs: its interior a delight; a proper snug; stained glass windows; truly magnificent ceiling and a Dansette record player providing the music. The beer is kept to the finest of standards, with a blend of ales from local breweries and carefully selected brews from further afield. It is a small, intimate establishment; it has the best of manners and expects and gets the same from its clientele. It employs the best of staff, true masters of their trade. Quite simply, there is nothing like it anymore.

Wallow in the atmosphere; let is wash over you. It is a place of warmth, both of spirit and kind. A place with 1000 stories soaked into its fabric. The author has stood in the bar with not another living soul present, yet has never felt alone. Long may it remain; it is an institution beyond measure.

There are frequent buses up the hill into the centre of the city and plenty of taxis. Having dined, the walker should rest up ready for the morrow; it will be a long but interesting day.

Cheers!

NEWCASTLE:
A DAY OF DISCOVERY

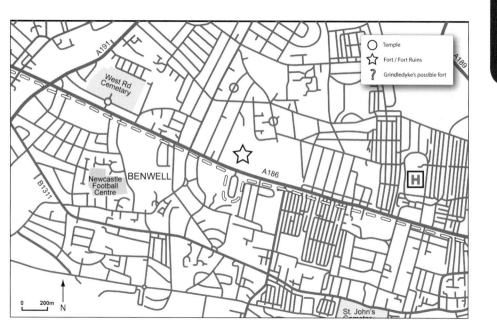

- **Soft shoes**
- **Purchase a return ticket on the Metro to Wallsend**
- **www.twmuseums.org.uk/segedunum**

START Monument–Manors–Byker–Chillingham Road–Walkergate–Wallsend **END**

Start the day after the Newcastle rush hour. No earlier than 9.30 a.m. for a reasonably priced ticket.

Use whichever Metro station is closest to you.

On arrival at Wallsend the walker will note that the Metro takes into account the importance of its Roman heritage, being the only railway station in the UK with signs in Latin. Follow the signs to Segedunum. Not far, a gentle stroll along Victorian streets that once heralded a coal-mining community next door to a busy shipbuilding area – what a contrast Segedunum is from its later Victorian surroundings.

Some years ago, when the author was asked for his opinion of the then brand-new Segedunum museum and viewing tower, he considered, he viewed and he described it as 'Looking like a badly sited airport terminal with an unfinished car park out the front.' This did not make him universally popular.

Please feel free to disagree with the author. He fully acknowledges the excellent idea of the viewing tower and the amount of space available for education parties and exhibitions, but is left cold by the very late twentieth-century architecture which dominates the remains.

Some useful information can be found at: www.dur.ac.uk/resources/ archaeological.services/research_training/hadrianswall_research_framework/ project_documents/Wallsend.pdf.

The Wall was extended from Pons Aelius Newcastle-upon-Tyne three years after the rest of the system was constructed; the reasoning for this is unclear, as is the reason why it stopped where it did.

However, do not be put off; this is an excellent site, worthy of spending some time over. Note the fort layout. The layout is that of the refurbishment under Emperor Severus in the late second and early third century. You will see other fort layouts along the way, but little or nothing from the Hadrianic period; refurbishment and redesign has buried much of the early works.

The viewing tower with its historical view assists in understanding the archaeological sequences and does supply a sense of timescale. Note that the north gate is jutting out into the territory beyond the Wall; this will be a particular feature elsewhere along the way.

The Wall abutted on to the south-western side of the fort and continued physically into the Tyne itself. It had three of the four fort gates opening on to the non-Roman side. The author is yet to be convinced of this as a terminus of the Wall, as he has already speculated at length elsewhere. It is the official terminus of the Hadrian's National Trail and the walker may well see other walkers finishing their journey from Bowness-on-Solway. As these tired walkers from Bowness-on-Solway started at a point looking out into the Irish

Sea, with the Solway to its right, it seems reasonable that this might just be the same case at the other end, rather than a river a good few kilometres from the North Sea. The author trusts that the walker understands the ground-breaking nature of this adventure.

Close to the outline of the Severan-period fort (which sits within the Hadrianic one) there is a recreation of a Roman bathhouse, which is excellent and it actually works – a great success. It has provided much valuable insight into the health of the Romans and the need for constant management of the facility. Let the fires go out and the temperature will drop; the result on the interior could be disastrous. To walk into a room with high windows that allow the light to float at its roof, to see a Roman gymnasium as it was originaly meant, to see baths that would have been a delight at the end of a cold day on the Wall – it is truly like stepping into a moment of the past.

The *vicus* and part of the fort is buried by the road that passes through the site. The possibilities for excavation to the north and east are likewise very limited, relying upon the occasional opportunity that building works and utility replacements afford. No sign of a ditch, palisade, wall or vallum has thus far been recorded in the immediate vicinity.

From Segedunum the walker has a choice: walk the busy A187 back into town (not recommended) or catch the Metro. For those wishing to walk, the details appear anon. Better to head for Newcastle by Metro – not that the author is trying to persuade.

Is this cheating?

Not at all; there are plenty of things to do and this is the last day in Newcastle before the real walking begins. More importantly, the walker is picking up valuable information to assist a better understanding of what they will see along the way.

For those anxious to take everything in, head along Buddle Road, through Walker on to Byker Hill; you can drop down and back up over the site of a possible bridge and ford of the Ouseburn and back up the other side; as the walker will not yet be aware, this can all be managed in a straight line.

See if you can find the way from Byker to this location:

OS Grid Reference: NZ2547464148
OS Grid Co-ordinates: 425474, 564148
Latitude/Longitude: 54.9713, -1.6036

This sits on top of the Wall; when you have found this site head for the Lit & Phil, as below.

For those not wanting the considerable hike from Wallsend to Newcastle, head for the Metro station and back into Newcastle; alight at Central Station.

The walker should proceed out of the main entrance and turn immediately right along the length of the station, past the Station Hotel; bear slightly left with the pavement and the Lit & Phil hoves into view.

▌Lit & Phil
www.litandphil.org.uk

You may enter and are most definitely very welcome; indeed your support for this institution is much required. The Lit & Phil is more than a library, it is a most liberal and enquiring institution, a place to enlighten the mind. It is a joy of a building and, like so many things full of joy, it is both bursting at the seams and finding it difficult to keep the parts as a whole. Your contribution to keeping the Lit & Phil as a beacon of learning in a fast-changing world is very much appreciated. At the time of writing the new cafe on the ground floor is going ahead, so let us hope it is open for the walker to enjoy.

The next building, and very much in contrast with the classical lines of the Lit & Phil, is Neville Hall, the home of the North of England Institute of Mining and Mechanical Engineers, a Victorian high gothic design of the best quality.

Note that there is an enclosure between the pavement and the building. This largely forgotten space contains the remains of Hadrian's Wall. Whilst Westgate takes you to the castle, the Wall is veering across the road away from our imaginary view.

Continue past Neville Hall, along Westgate, in the shadow of the railway and, after crossing some quite busy side roads, you will reach the Black Gate.

15 The Lit & Phil, Newcastle. Worth a second glance – go in, they don't bite

The edifice under the railway bridge to the right, as the walker crosses the road junction, is Robert Stephenson's high-level bridge, an engineering wonder as great as the day it was built in 1847, carrying road on one level and rail on another. The positioning of the bridge creates a triangular junction of the lines to the south with the line to Edinburgh and the north, with the keep sitting between two. The castle keep provides a piece of engineering symbolism; Newcastle is physically part of the advancement of the Victorian age.

The author recommends a short diversion to enjoy this engineering marvel.

Having enjoyed the view and the fantastic ironwork, it is time to head back to the castle.

These are the very substantial remains of the castle gatehouse, much altered since its construction in 1247.

Until very recently it was the home of the Society of Antiquaries of Newcastle-upon-Tyne, now moved to the Hancock Museum; the walker will be heading there later.

DAY 2

▌Society of Antiquaries, Newcastle-upon-Tyne
www.newcastle-antiquaries.org.uk

The present keep was constructed in 1172, replacing earlier more flammable versions, and can be reached by popping underneath the arches. Under some you will see the only known remains of the Roman fort.

Take time to explore and get a feel for the castle's position, overlooking the river, where the Pons Aelius could be constructed. Impose the fort design the walker has just seen at Wallsend upon the scene; remove the keep and the railway, and you are left with a near cliff face on the south and eastern side, with a playing-card-shaped fort sitting handsomely upon it. An imposing, very daunting site, commanding respect from all that approached this important crossing of ways – the major north–south road and the River Tyne.

The Wall doesn't physically connect to the fort, it passes slightly to the north of the site, roughly just to the south of the very fine Old Post Office. The author finds this very curious, especially as the site of Pons Aelius was initially considered a terminus, but this is not the only anomaly to be explored.

The original terminus at Pons Aelius actually creates problems for the engineering of the extension to Segedunum. The Wall could go further inland than it does, which would ease the crossing of the Ouseburn, rather than having the wide crossing down by the river. The fort guards on the river crossing the Wall slightly to the north could have been even further north and then angled east with a new gate appropriate for the through traffic; this would have allowed for an expansion of the space to the north for a *vicus* away from the river front. There appears to have been no effort to do so, which is odd; the whole Roman site seems to be very squeezed in, and not just because of later building works.

Note the steep slope, especially towards the east where Dog Leap Steps takes the walker down to Side. These steps are very steep and sometimes slippery when wet. If you don't fancy them, walk around the Black Gate and down the cobbled road to meet them at the bottom.

Pass the Crown Posada, unless it is opening time, in which case the walker should take advantage of the opportunity for a glass or two of refreshing ale. Archaeological research is thirsty work and the mind requires lubrication on a regular basis.

Bear slightly right past Betty Surtee's house (worth a look) to the T-junction. Look to the left across the river, where there is the swing bridge. It is worthy of further exploration in its own right, but with respect to Roman investigations it is the exact spot where the Pons Aelius stood, much of which was recovered when the swing bridge was being constructed. Line the bridge up with the castle remains high above. There are steps up from the river to the castle mound, but the author does not recommend them, especially at night.

16 Side of the swing bridge – 'cos it is canny lad!'

It is very obvious that you would not be able to proceed further north without being noticed; likewise a ship coming up the Tyne would be seen from a considerable distance. As the bridge would act as the terminus for ships, there would have to be transhipment to smaller vessels hereabouts, so the area immediately around Side would have seen much activity. The present quay is the result of much later shipping activity, the marshy lands being reclaimed by use of spent ballast from ships slowly but surely developing the quay that is seen today. There is some evidence that there was a formal military presence on the Gateshead side of the bridge; more work needs to be done to identify its purpose.

The author suggests that the walker takes a stroll along the quay and enjoys the scene; it is worth the diversion: day or night the quay and its bridges are an impressive site. The Baltic Centre enthrals and irritates the author in equal measure; it therefore is doing its job well enough and should the walker wish to stray for a few hours it is worthy of the time. The lift bridge is also worth viewing, especially if it does actually lift (which is not that often).

However, if the walker is to keep to a reasonable timetable, after a short adventure on the quay they should head back up to the Black Gate and back along Westgate Road. Keep on Westgate Road, rather than going to the railway station (which is on Neville Street); negotiate your way westward through the traffic courtesy of plenty of pedestrian crossings, until you get to the Newcastle Arts Centre at number 67.

This is a fantastic spot, even more so when the walker realises that there is a milecastle beneath and that they can still view part of it. The walker should head for the Black Swan Courtyard and David Fry Ceramics.

⚠ This is not an environment for heavy backpacks; ceramics of great artistry and worth prefer to be whole and the walker's pocket not lightened by accident.

Newcastle Arts Centre
www.newcastle-arts-centre.co.uk
David Fry Ceramics
http://davidfryceramics.com/archive/archaeology

There is something very odd about this milecastle; it mucks up all the numbering sequences for the rest of the Wall. The author has previously warned of the numbering system. Its presence also calls into account the likelihood of two others ever being built. The problem being that there is a misconstrued, half-hearted belief that the Romans always adhered to a strict code of construction and to plans. The reality is that they obeyed them wherever possible and used common sense the rest of the time; the ever-practical Roman engineer could solve any problem, but only if it served a purpose to do so. The Wall is undoubtedly an example of instruction followed, but also of adjusting to the practicalities on the ground.

Those walkers interested in the numbering sequences for turrets and milecastles should keep in the back of their minds where the Wall or frontier actually starts: Tynemouth or Wallsend? It makes a difference.

Having fully perused the arts centre, the author can recommend a destination for lunch: the Newcastle Arms, 57 St Andrews Street, next to Chinatown – a well-respected city pub, offering a very fine selection of ales. There are many other excellent establishments; the author only offers his personal choice, but no doubt the walker will have their own. Chinatown is great for lunch, the businesses vying with each other to get the walker through the door – take your time and get a bargain. Rest and enjoy the city.

Repast complete, and if starting from the Newcastle Arms, turn right out of the pub and left at the bottom of the road; straight across at the roundabout and along Percy Street (not the most attractive of Newcastle city-centre streets). Go past the Hotspur pub on to Barras Bridge with the university on your left; pass the bookshop and the excellent little sandwich bar. Turn left on to Claremont Road and follow the signs for the Great North Museum and the Hancock.

The Great North Museum is a must see, if only because of the interactive model of Hadrian's Wall. But there is much more. This is an opportunity for the walker to find out about Mithras and Coventina's Well; these two separate subjects will be very useful in the next few days and will give no small insight into the Roman world. If the walker has difficulty finding information on either subject just ask.

▌Great North Museum
www.twmuseums.org.uk/greatnorthmuseum

The author would be surprised if the walker will be out of the museum in less than two hours. There is much to see and do.

Ask what happened in Newcastle-upon-Tyne at half past midnight on 6 October 1854.

Now for the walker's first practical test. Did the author forget to mention there would be a test? How remiss. It must be his age, he could have sworn he mentioned it, but no matter a test there will be. The task is to get to Benwell Roman fort (Condercum) by public transport. This lesson will come in useful for later in the walk. For those that are using a PDA or smart phone, the following site will be of use: www.transportdirect.info. Start at NE2 4PT and end at NE15 6QN. Buy a Return.

Various bus services run to Benwell from the city centre. For those without digital aids, walk to the bus stop you will have passed on the way into the Hancock Museum, on the same side of the road as the museum. Catch a number 10 and alight at the nearest bus stop to Denhill Park on West Road, which is slap bang inside the fort. Now find the vallum crossing and small Roman temple.

The fact that this exercise is in a busy city with plenty of people to ask makes it a relatively easy one; yet if you are a stranger it is still quite daunting. Better to get to grips with acquainting the walker with buses in a city where there are plenty of them and people to ask. It would be unfair to be trying out the walker's skills on an exposed stretches of Wall often with only a single chance of a bus back to civilisation!

Why is the author making this point?

As much of the Wall is an exposed lonely place, depending on when the walker decides to cross there maybe few people about; there is always a need to have a plan B available and timing can be an essential to reach a warm bed for the night.

Why not walk?

The author would suggest that it would be more fulfilling to get a bus to Benwell; if for no better reason than that it

17 Newcastle pride

emphasises its urban location. The fort is lost to view under the reservoir, offices and houses; however, it remains relatively intact below the house foundations and only partially damaged by the office block. Most of the fort was on the south side of the Wall, with only one gate on the north side. The vallum is very well presented and this is the first time the walker has had a view of it since Wallsend. Indeed, except for a few stones under a railway viaduct at the castle, these are the only Roman remains the walker has seen since Wallsend.

The fortunate feature regarding Benwell is the presence of the inquisitive antiquarian that got to the spot before Newcastle-upon-Tyne needed a better water supply. Plenty of inscriptions have survived and a reasonable idea of the internal layout was gathered. Yet again, the barracks seemed not to have been able to house the troops adequately that, by the inscriptions found at the site (thus providing a link between structure and date), should have been present. In this case a tombstone found nearby:

> D M S D IVLIVS Q F CANDIDVS CHO PVANGIONVM A XXXX
> To the holy spirits of the departed Decimus Iulius Candidus, son of Quintus, of
> the First Cohort of Vangiones, forty years

The Vangiones were a Belgic tribe originating from the upper Rhine. The First Cohort of Vangiones was a mixed unit of both horse and foot soldiers, a *cohors equitata*, and officially there were 1000 personnel (*cohors milliaria*), which suggests most were living outside of the fort walls, as the walker will encounter elsewhere along the way.

The little Roman temple is to the god Antenociticus, a native god venerated by the Romans. Religions were of great interest to the Romans; they collected them like stamps and had a very practical attitude towards deities, rites and ritual practices: if it worked and didn't involve human sacrifice or frighten the horses or endanger the emperor, then it was OK. For the Roman military, taking part and carrying out strict ritual processes came easily; they took orders well, obeyed and understood the need for preciseness. This is a very small temple (and the author suggests that the walker stands in it – when he was last there it was permitted) allowing for the robed officiate and perhaps two assistants, an entrance screen to keep the bustle of the *vicus* out and provide a darkened space. There would be precious little room for the devotions of those wishing the assistance of the god. Any animal or bird sacrifice would be likely to splatter all present.

Antenociticus appears to have been popular, but only at Benwell, considering the inscriptions thanking him for the resultant promotions. It has made the author wonder about him – is it possible that this god was merely a simple but effective money-earning machine? The temple's location, right next to the fort, is a busy commercial spot; it makes the author think of a seaside fortune teller's booth. He is probably wrong, but why doesn't Antenociticus turn up elsewhere on the Wall?

The head of the Antenociticus was found in 1862; the body was probably wood. It is notable for its full head of flowing hair.

The contrast between the temple and *vallum* and the present-day surroundings is extreme. It is as if they have landed from another planet, whereas, of course, we have landed on theirs. The author suspects they will see off all the buildings around them and triumph over the landscape for a few more thousand years yet.

Time for a final test of map-reading skills. Find this listed structure, which is pretty obvious:

OS Grid Reference: NZ2072164222
OS Grid Co-ordinates: 420721, 564222
Latitude/Longitude: 54.9722, -1.6778

Without this listed structure Newcastle would not have been able to grow; it is an integral part of the machinery of how a city worked. Waterworks are not new; the walker will encounter others along the way – but without chimneys.

Time to head back into Newcastle to provision up for the journey ahead; plenty of high-energy snacks and refreshment in the Crown Posada would no doubt aid the planning.

18 Dog Leap Steps – 'Mind How You Go!'

DAY 2

DAY 3

NEWCASTLE TO THE PORT GATE

- **Early start, by 9 a.m. at the latest**
- **Light, soft shoes needed (change later in the day)**
- **Terrain: flat, easy-going, mostly road and pavement**

The author will from time to time vary from the Hadrian's National Trail and include a bit of road walking. The walker can be trusted to use their common sense. Depending on the walker, weather conditions and daylight, this is a maximum of 30km day. The longest of the lot!

The author will start this walk at Benwell; the walker may decide to walk out to this spot if they so wish. Just keep a good pace up otherwise you will fall behind.

The road is the Wall from the western side of the fort and the walker will note that both begin a relatively steep descent towards the Denton Burn; keep to the south side of the road.

If the walker is using an ordnance map, the vallum is clearly marked and the Wall is marked where possible along the road. The landscape is domestic and suburban; the road is busy, fast and uncomfortable. Some walkers may consider that a bus out to Denton Burn would have been a better bet, but the surroundings are as much a history of the Wall as anything else. This is the development of Newcastle in the twentieth century; the sprawl of a mighty city. The housing is quite substantial and mostly dates from a period before 1929. Benwell fort had been used as a reservoir in 1862 to deal with the expansion of the city; the hamlet of Denton Burn was swallowed with a single gulp within 40 years of that.

Fortunately, as the Wall had been a constant in the scenery it was a physical and therefore an available useful structure. It survived to be well recorded into the twentieth century, deliberately so because it was obvious that it would be submerged by the expansion of the city.

The roar of traffic increases as the walker continues down the slope into Denton Burn and the curry house is worth a look at for just a tiny bit of Wall – somebody bothered to look after it. The Wall announces itself with a neatly grassed area with restored stonework, the highest bit since Wallsend and no doubt quite a relief for the walker. The burn was crossed by the Wall in a substantially constructed conduit, now somewhere under the ramp of the foot over-bridge.

The roar of the traffic increases again and the A11 is reached; over the top of this continuing roar and Denton Hall turret is met, along with a good stretch of restored wall. The setting clearly shows that until the twentieth

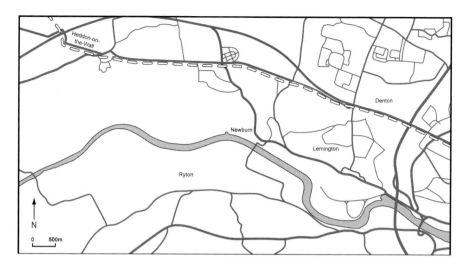

century this was countryside, down a slope, rather than on the higher ground to the right.

The walker will note that the atmosphere changes as you enter West Denton. The traffic noise still fills the air, but the houses are further back. The Wall is parallel to the A69. The author trusts that the walker will notice that things feel less hectic the moment the A11 is crossed. It is possible to relax and let the countryside slowly in, because the A69 heads a little to the north and the Wall and the road to Throckley heads left. Follow the Wall on the B6528.

Chapel House Farm had a milecastle, fully recorded. The walker will note that the author does not point all milecastles out; he will do so in this case as this particular one has completely vanished. It lasted until at least 1928.

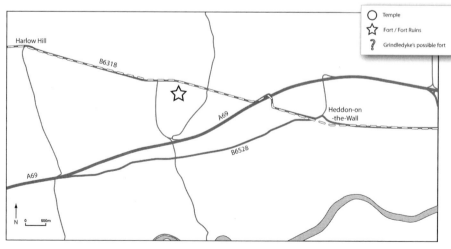

Wallbottle is soon reached. The vallum is very clear, running parallel to the pavement. The name of the village means 'Dwelling on the Wall'. The road is busy, the going easy and the occasional glimpse of the past keeps the spirits high. Throckley is the next target in this neat little suburb, but the hill provides a little exercise which is rewarded by a good long length of Wall hoving into view. There is a hidden gem hereabouts, but it takes some finding. The vallum is thickly covered in gorse; if the walker can penetrate it at the crest of the hill there is a section of vallum cut through solid rock. This is not for the faint hearted, but the marks of the Romans' efforts are still clearly visible in the rock face. The author has looked for *graffiti*, but to no avail. You may be luckier, it's worth a look.

The Wall is tall here and very well presented; there is a great deal of local pride in the Wall. Note the medieval kiln built into the Wall; you will notice much re-use of the Wall from here on.

Heddon-on-the-Wall
www.english-heritage.org.uk/daysout/properties/heddon-on-the-wall-hadrians-wall

Three Tuns Inn
1 Military Road
Heddon-on-the-Wall
Newcastle-upon-Tyne
NE15 0BQ
Tel: 01661 852172

Heddon-on-the-Wall village offers refreshment; the author enjoys the Three Tuns Inn. The next section is markedly exposed and the walker should make sure that they have wet-weather kit ready. For the first time in the walk bovines outnumber the humans.

Out of Heddon along the B6138 the pavement gets a tad narrow; look over the stone wall and the vallum is in plain view. The walker will have wondered why the road they are traversing is so well built; understandably the Roman wall beneath assists and that is because one General George Wade found it a jolly good foundation for his military road between Heddon and Greenhead in 1746. Wade, famous for his road and fort building in the Highlands in the 1720s, was somewhat out of favour in 1745, when he failed to stop that well-known Italian, Bonnie Prince Charlie, and his merry porridge eaters from making an attempt to get to London to overthrow a Hanoverian king. In fact, Wade was sacked for his inability to stop the invasion; he had a good excuse: there were no proper roads across the country. Thus he was given the task of bringing the system up to the standards he had installed in the Highlands. His death in 1748 probably saved further Wall destruction. However, allowing for the destruction of the Wall since 1748 and Wade's efforts especially, as much of the Wall will actually have survived beneath the modern tarmac – not that bad.

There is a short diversion for the A69 improvements; beware the road. Take the signposted National Trail, Hadrian's Wall footpath.

There is a milecastle at 55.001399°N 1.819958°W, the last before Rudchester (Vindobala); the walker has passed over the top of the associated turret not long before. Turrets and their positioning are another minefield of numbering; the structures are more important in the main than the modern numerical sequence. Their purpose was to provide raised observation platforms and internal shelter for the troops. Denton Hall turret has provided a very reasonable example, but needless to say they do vary and they do get rebuilt, not always on the same site that keep the number crunchers happy.

Rudchester is soon reached; it is not that obvious.

The fort straddles the Wall with three of its gates to the north. It has a *mithraeum* outside its south-eastern walls, the contents of which are now in the Great North Museum. It had a long and venerable life seeing alterations, suggesting a continued military adherence to Mithras. The author ponders if this temple may once have contained an alternative god, that of Jupiter Doliches, and was converted later to Mithras.

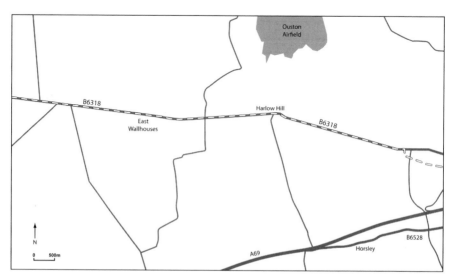

There was a *vicus* at Rudchester, to the south-west, and this would have housed ex-servicemen with skills, wives and partners of the troops. A handy spot to stop when marching the Wall, no doubt; but there is no ease or refreshment today and the walker must pass by. It is a pity that interpretation boards do not give distances to the nearest ale house.

The Wall keeps upon its straight path to March Burn; the way is good, but cars and tractors make for the odd foray into the modern ditch. The walker will now just about be able to identify the lumps and bumps of the Wall and vallum, so the leftward slant of the road should be a clue. It coincides with a milecastle and the preparation of the engineers to straddle Eppies Hill. Here we meet the theorists and postulators; there should be a turret hereabouts and the vallum is very present.

Harlow Hill is a good stroll away and the vallum stays an ever constant, but the approach to Harlow Hill shows clear indication of a complex earthwork. It is a milecastle and one very nicely placed, which allows for a jolly good view all the way back across an open landscape of neat, large fields and the reservoir to the right. The vallum is close to the Wall and exceedingly deep as the walker descends the hill. Keep along the way, but beware the traffic. There being long, straight stretches, the speed tends to be high. There is a good amount of level verge along the way.

Fortunately, the Robin Hood Inn appears on the scene, where very good food can be had, much needed after such exertions. The Robin Hood is staffed by helpful, friendly people with a mission to add several centimetres to the waistline. There is accommodation here.

▌ Robin Hood Inn
www.robinhoodnorthumberland.co.uk

The walker has travelled 24km as far as this point.

Be aware that it is 9.6km to Corbridge from here. The time of day and the season may make it sensible to call a taxi from Corbridge and restart in the morning.

▌ Taxi Companies
http://geofftate.350.com/page-2.htm
Tel: 07958 040163
www.advancedtaxis.com
Tel: 01434 606565

If the weather and light is good, the feet in tip-top form, and the walker has the will, there are some interesting bits of archaeology to see here.

If starting in the morning the Robin Hood Inn is the start point.

The vallum widens considerably after the Robin Hood Inn, markedly so, as if a different set of chaps were working on the job; it would make a jolly good canal in parts. The author would like to state that this is a joke – he does not wish to add to the multitude of theories regarding the vallum!

Can you find the milecastle at the road junction for Matfen?

As you enter Halton Shields, it soon becomes apparent that the milecastle is not going to be open to view; it lies underneath twentieth-century housing: www.pastscape.org/hob.aspx?hob_id=20464.

The pavement is the place to be, which is easy enough walking, and the National Trail is well marked. Over the top of Down Hill the walker can step off the path and take in the Wall and vallum in detail, as the road and Wall part company. The Wall heads south-west and goes straight on over the top of the road, the vallum goes round, and the two join again after the hill. It will come as no surprise that there is a milecastle here.

The fort of Halton Chesters (Onno or Onnum or Hunuum) sits as a series of uninterpreted lumps, bumps and pasture; yet it is of considerable importance. Not because it is large – indeed, it is, and also an odd shape with an extension on the southern side of the Wall, not continued on the northern. The odd factor is the presence of Dere Street, the main Roman road to Scotland, which passes within less than 1.4km. It seems logical to put the two features together, especially as any major road going through the Wall would have required military administration and structure. It may be that as there was a major civilian settlement (*vicus*) between the fort and Dere Street, that any idea of diverting the road closer to or moving the site of the fort was deemed a waste of effort.

Archaeology of the Port Gate seems a tad thin on the ground, but it has been assisted recently with a significant find: the contents of a late Romans purse (http://finds.org.uk/blogs/northeast/2007/09/18/hadrian-wall). In particular, a *Gloria Romanorum* (coin) dated to AD 406. Judging by the state of it, it had been in use for a while, suggesting that the Wall and its organisation was still functioning right to the end of direct Roman rule in 410, and possibly into the post-Roman era, when the locals were starting to look after themselves and the Roman coinage system hung on as a tenuous link with the old regime.

This find was the result of a member of the public reporting his discovery to the Portable Antiquities Service. Please visit their website (http://finds.org. uk) and use their services if you find an item in the landscape.

Halton Castle (NY997679) presents a worthy diversion. It is easily reached from Halton Chester and has been the recipient of the Wall and fort's stone for its much rebuilt fourteenth-century tower house with Jacobean extension. The earthworks are that of an enclosure, known as a barmekin; a cattle enclosure perhaps, or a defensive barrier; it would serve as both.

With a pub and archaeological site right next door, the author thinks this is an excellent opportunity for a long-term project.

Back on the tarmac again, the walker needs to take care on the gentle right-hand bend as the verge is narrow. The vallum is clearly visible over the Wall to the left.

In the short distance between Halton Chester and the Port Gate the turret seems to have met a fate courtesy of the gods: it appears to have been destroyed by a lightning bolt. In 1850 a stone marked *Fulgar divom* (lightning of the gods) was found, and the turret had indeed been rebuilt and resited. Perhaps the gods agreed with the author regarding the numbering sequence!

The Errington Arms stands just to the south of the junction between the Wall going east to west, and Dere Street going south to north.

DAY 3

▌ The Errington Arms

www.erringtonarms.co.uk

From here the walker should head for a bed for the night. Hexham and Corbridge are easily reached from here, from the bus stop opposite the pub. It is 16 minutes to Hexham by bus. Allowing for a connection in Hexham, add 11 minutes to Corbridge.

There are no late buses. If needed use the taxi number as per Robin Hood Inn.

The walker will have travelled 30km; this is the longest distance in a day for walking in the entire adventure.

A DIVERSION

The author has wandered the Wall for more years than he really wishes to remember, but by good judgement a period of three years at Newcastle University meant the Wall was a very close neighbour.

The author does not do camping; it seems odd when there is always a pub or a B&B somewhere nearby or, better still, a farmhouse and a friendly person that can rustle up a comfy bed and a good breakfast at a very reasonable rate.

However, time and research can override comfort and the author admits on this occasion he was attempting a tad too much research in too little time, and the only answer was to spend a few hours under canvas. In this case, his trusty plastic sheet made for a reasonable groundsheet, tent and finds-sorting area (you can wash it down afterwards). Having spent a most enjoyable evening in a pub near Dere Street the author headed to his hideaway for the night.

Always plan in advance; that is the key. Sleeping in ditches is not to be recommended; they are damp, uncomfortable and you won't be allowed in the pub the next day!

Having organised a shelter against the only bit of wall about, by putting the edge of his plastic sheet between some stones that had once been part of the Wall, the author prepared for the night. Using his waterproof as a blanket and his backpack as a pillow, he settled down for the night. He did not expect much sleep; previous experiences had shown that cat napping was the only way to get through the small hours. This would be no different, no doubt.

The night sky can be stunning and this night was no exception: warm and clear, not a sound. The author, having checked for livestock before setting up, only expected the snuffling of badgers and the ghastly cry of foxes. What he got was rather different.

Time passed, as it does, but in a lazy sort of way, especially when sleep does not come easily because of the change of environment, the beer and the plans for the morrow. So the distant sound of sandpaper on wood was enough to perk him up and out of his dismal sleeping mode.

Not wishing to move from his quite comfortable position (anyone that has camped knows the delight of finding the right sleeping position and the merest movement can wreck it), he lay and listened. It was a very odd sound and it was getting louder; there was a distinct beat to it and a jangle as well. A one, two, three, four, a one, two, three, four; a swaying tramp, tramp, tramp with a distinct clang on the first beat.

The sound got louder, much louder, and the author pushed the light on his watch; it proved that he was awake. He lay, listening to the marching; it ticked on, the sound of horses' hooves, snorting, a wheeled vehicle, another, creaking along. Then nothing, absolutely nothing; stillness, the night enveloped it all.

The whole experience had lasted over ten minutes; the fact that it had not faded away was the most frightening part, the sudden stop, like flicking a switch. Up to then fascination was the only emotion. Whilst there was noise there was continuity, but once gone it left only a void, which was filled, quite naturally, by fear. There was to be no sleep after that.

In comparison with some experiences the author has had in broad daylight on archaeological sites (especially when his father was in command), it would rate about 3/10. But they are stories for another day.

 Such camping is much frowned upon by all parties, so take this as a stern warning not to do it. The Wall environment is constantly 'on the edge' and the flora and fauna have enough to cope with without humans making things even worse for them.

DAY 3

DAY 4

THE PORT GATE TO CHESTERS

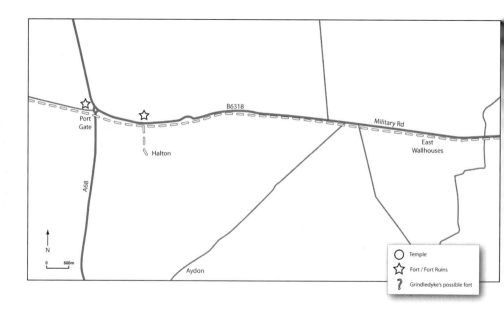

- **Early start essential, 8.30 a.m. at the latest**
- **Walking boots necessary**
- **Terrain: tarmac, gravel and grass**

Depending on where the walker spent the night the intention of today is to take a break from the Wall and travel from the Port Gate to Corbridge. This can be done on foot or by bus from the bus stop opposite the Errington Arms.

Those that have spent the night in Hexham will have enjoyed a very good fish and chip shop next to the abbey. There is an extremely fine Roman gravestone in the abbey, *Ala Petriana*, *Flavinus*, which deserves attention, especially in respect to the Roman attitude to some of the natives.

This tombstone, along with many other pieces of Roman stone, has made its way along the river and up the hill. More anon.

The author recommends the Tap & Spile for refreshment; it also offers accomodation.

Tap & Spile
Battle Hill
Town Centre
Hexham NE46 2EB
Tel: 0871 917 0007

Hexham has a considerable amount to offer: the old gaol, the abbey full of Roman stone from Corbridge and, most interesting of all, the seventh-century crypt, which is built out of Roman monumental stone, much of which came from the Roman bridge at Corbridge. If there is one structure you should visit off the Wall, it is this. The crypt was designed to contain relics and is built with great skill; the visitor is in darkness and then after turning two right-hand turns is enlightened at the shrine, which would have been richly decorated, a deliberate contrast to emphasise the importance of the relics within.

St Wilfrid, responsible for the construction, had visited Rome and, having seen the way Christianity could be presented, he brought the concept back with him. As this was the seventh century and Christianity was still trying to get a hold, any promotional opportunity had to be taken, especially if those visiting were willing to make a donation.

DAY 4

19 Detail of Hexham gaol

Things have not changed today to this day, and it is certainly worth the effort – do give generously.

The author hopes walkers will manage to convene at:

54.975311 N -2.029252 W
Corbridge Roman Town
NE45 5NT

As this is an English Heritage site a charge is made. The interpretation is good and the two granaries and the town centre give a sense of scale and importance. There is a great deal more of the site outside the fence under the grass.

Corbridge and its immediate environs are the site of more than one fort – indeed, this is a very complicated place – but the element of outstanding importance is that it is the site of a river crossing. Everything else arises from this fact; anywhere an army can safely cross a river will become a significant spot, it is the way of things. Water isn't just a liquid to the Romans, it signifies a place of the gods; due payment has to be made and respects given.

Corbridge Roman Bridge

www.twmuseums.org.uk/archaeology/our-projects/corbridge-roman-bridge.html

Corbridge Roman site is a very complex place. A concise archaeological history of works is available here: www.dur.ac.uk/resources/archaeological.services/research_training/hadrianswall_research_framework/project_documents/Corbridge.pdf

There is even more: a lost mausoleum, a destroyed bathhouse, at least two more forts nearby. All this is happening just at the bottom of the hill from the Wall; Corbridge pre-dating the Wall is a vital part of it and the Roman control of the north.

Modern Corbridge is a pretty spot; there are a number of fine public houses and an excellent Indian curry house at the railway station some way out of the town.

For those requiring quality retail therapy, Corbridge is hard to beat. Delightful window dressings entice the browser in, while myriad artisan wares and highly original products allow Corbridge to punch well above its weight in respect of shopping. You will want to return.

Dyvel's Inn
www.dyvelsinn.co.uk

The atmosphere and friendly staff are enough to make the walker consider staying an extra day.

Allowing for a good look round, it is time to get back to the Port Gate.

Take the bus from Corbridge to Stagshaw Roundabout. At the time of writing there is a frequent service to Stagshaw, via Hexham. Those not wishing to have the diversion can take a fast car – there are taxis more than willing to assist at reasonable cost.

Walking starts again here. Just before the Errington Arms take the National Trail Hadrian's Wall path to the left; the ditch is very clear and, as ever, the Wall itself is well beneath the walker's boots. Taking the opportunity to get off the road here to walk the National Trail takes the strain off the ankles and soles. This is an easy way to start a walk, especially on a hot day; the plantation offers some shade, then open rolling countryside, the vallum seeming to be just a ruffle of the turf. There is marvellous sledging in the winter as long as you don't hit the oak trees – but that is a story for another day. The vallum then begins to widen and then deepen, the tree cover becomes a memory and milecastle 24 is reached. The author mentions it because it is very obvious. For the walker they should be at the entrance to High Errington Farm.

If not, where are you?

The vallum gets serious there; some massive effort has been put into this section. This is spade and wicker basket work, wide enough for wagons and horses. The dreaded gorse takes hold of the vallum; fortunately it seems that its spread is being checked. It is pretty, but a menace to cattle and archaeologists alike.

The walker will note a church on a hill, St Oswalds, which is worth a second look and a diversion. This is the believed site of the battle between Oswald and Cadwallon of Gwynedd and King Penda of Mercia; Cadwallon and Penda were out to finish off the Northumbrian kingdom that had already mauled and divided. Bede's account of Oswald having a vision the night before the battle has a remarkable similarity to what is supposed to have happened to Constantine before the battle of the Milvian Bridge in Rome (AD 312), including all the non-Christians on Oswald's side agreeing to become Christian if they won.

Note that the Wall is not on the top of this high point but runs along the lower contour; a case of building tidily and quickly rather overtly, which is the case elsewhere.

According to Bede and others the Cadwallon and Penda force arrived at the Port Gate, turned right and came unstuck trying to get Oswald off the hill by approaching him along the ridge.

The walker should look at the map: locate Dere Street and then consider the options. The most obvious features on the landscape are the hills and rolling slopes, water and boggy patches. Dere Street is the fast route and easy going under foot, on the approach to Port Gate, but then things would get a tad awkward for someone intent on attack.

There is a route from Dere Street to Oswald's high point that is much more advantageous. From Dere Street turn left to Hempstead Farm, proceed to Sandhoe, then to Fawcett Hill, which gives a very good view of Oswald's movement, then to Coldaw Hill, which would act as a very good vantage and rallying point directly in line with Oswald. This is a much better approach than fighting over Whittington Fell.

Cadwallon and Penda may have divided forces; a mistake and they were probably in too much of a hurry.

Oswald won because he couldn't be dislodged and he had the advantage of the remains of the Wall; the Port Gate and the Wall itself, even in a decrepit state, would act as a barrier – the vallum likewise.

The major problem for the Wall walker is that it vanishes at this point. There seems to be a kink here; the road moves from the Wall for its foundation over to where the vallum should and stays on the vallum until after the lane to Chesterwood, where, descending the bank, the previous arrangement returns. This is probably a result of Wade respecting Church land and the site of the battle.

An ancient cross was found near the church, probably of medieval date, although experts cannot agree on this; certainly the victory of Oswald created a resolve on the part of the Northumbrians to stand up for themselves and gave Christianity a better footing. Even after Oswald was killed (AD 642) the religion acted as a focal point and the Northumbrians recovered.

The author wonders if there is a fort hereabouts. There is something not right – the milecastles get in a muddle in their numbering sequence (which will keep some busy) and the landscape makes the author uneasy. With the years archaeologists begin to get a feel for things.

There are six unusual burn marks in the field to the south: pyres for the dead after the Welsh and Mercians came to a sticky end?

COWS

The National Trail provides a very pleasant way, a delight, but beware of the curious bovines.

Cattle should be treated with respect; do not disturb them, especially if they have calves, which they will naturally wish to protect.

Never run away from a cow. If a cow decides to approach you with an enthusiastic intent, no doubt just to say 'hello', but the speed of that enthusiasm worries, then raise one's arm and give a good hearty yell.

Continue to flap arms and walk towards the cow. The reaction is usually one of astonishment and a cessation of the desire to come closer. Never ever run.

Another milecastle and the last before a major and unexpected change lies beneath the sod and tarmac around NY93116953.

At last some physical remains are reached: the Wall remerges, a tattered fragment, the remains left when enough stone had been removed to assist building new barns and houses throughout the district. Fortunately, this is also the point where one of the major changes in the Wall takes place; it gets narrower. The Wall does vary in width throughout its length, but up to this point it has been 3m; at this point it drops to 2.5m.

Why the change?

It would save on stone and effort.

The location, in the middle of nowhere in particular, suggests it was a deliberate act, the result of an immediate instruction. Why suddenly were time and effort at a premium? There was no great uprising in the empire; the quality of the work remains as high; effort and stone supplies, and the distance and time for these seem to have been of little concern.

The author muses that a guard rail on the change would be a necessity. But, seriously, there is a case for considering that the Wall was nothing more than imperial show. Nobody is going to batter it down, and the half metre makes not one jot of difference – this change takes place in the middle of nowhere because that is the obvious place to do it; where nobody will notice. It saves the time and effort that the emperor is quite willing to expend, but the army can spend in more comfortable pursuits.

Archaeologically we cannot prove that the Wall top at this spot actually changed in width; that is to say, it is feasible that the walkway had a wooden

DAY 4

broad walk supported by timbers projecting directly out from the top of the Wall as the overhang would not have been immense. Thus the practical walking area would have remained standard. Wood is softer under foot than stone and potentially less slippery.

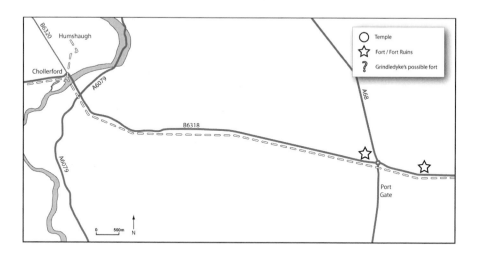

There you are! Archaeological theory, without a pint of beer anywhere in sight!

The walker can now enjoy the shade of the woods as the Wall descends the hill towards the Tyne. Brunton turret is soon reached and the walker can imagine the Romans enjoying this sentry post on a sunny day; the scene is delightful. No doubt the soldiers would have been looking forward to getting off duty, going fishing and a perhaps later a frolic with girlfriends down by the river. The river was much closer to the Brunton side than it is today; much has changed. This includes a recorded strange mound, considered initially to be a tumulus, but no burial was ever found. All traces have gone. The author wonders if it was a survey platform to allow the Roman surveyors to work out the complexities of the river crossing.

Can you spot Milecastle 27?

Methinks that will keep the number crunchers busy. Tick it off if you can see it.

Follow the National Trail markers and turn left at the crossroads in Low Brunton. Note there are some excellent remains of the railway station (Chollerford) here; the line ran from a junction west of Hexham to Riccarton Junction. However, passenger services were withdrawn in 1956 and completely shut down in 1959, save for a section at Bellingham.

Over the bridge into Chollerford and the grand expanse of the George Hotel sits to the right. Enjoy the view.

The walker should then turn left at the roundabout and in a very short distance left again into Chesters (Cilurnum) Roman fort. Here the walker can immerse themselves in a well-presented Roman site. The great river bridge foundations (mostly later than Hadrian) are of considerable worth, but the cup of tea is even better.

The bridge and the Wall pre-date the fort, the bridge undergoing several major reworkings over its life and the Wall, sitting beneath the fort, demolished to make way for it. The mortar can hardly have set before the fort emerged and the author can imagine some annoyance on the part of the engineers responsible for it. There are some questions to answer here. Why the sudden need for a full-blown military establishment that hadn't been considered important when the Wall was designed? The river is a substantial feature in the landscape, a major thoroughfare for military traffic, and no doubt some civilians as well; there would have to be protection at either end but it obviously wasn't considered that significant initially, unless the need to complete the imperial project was seen as more important than the practicalities.

The author considers the area around Chesters significant; it is a good place to build a bridge – the eastern and western banks are much more reasonable than some river crossings along the Wall. The bridge allows for a major east–west connection with Corbridge and its main York to Edinburgh route, Dere Street. Importantly, it is a point that is just about fordable at certain times of year and was thus in use before the Roman establishment. The author does not recommend trying this, but he has walked across both Tyne rivers in summer without the water coming above his thighs; on one occasion, not even to his knees.

It comes as no surprise that a fort was established here, not just to maintain strict control of a river crossing (the size is positively overkill for the task), but to control through-Wall traffic to the north.

The author believes that before the Wall was built a temporary annexation frontier segregating tribes reached across the east–west divide, and rather than cross the North Tyne at Chesters it crossed slightly further north between Haughton castle and Barrasford, then headed directly up to High Rochester, from where it headed onwards towards the Solway Firth. At Barrasford it is a very short distance to connect to Dere Street and thus Corbridge – a very handy short-cut if the traveller wished to head west and not go via Corbridge.

The order to construct the Wall takes no notice of this route initially and blocks the way, but the realisation that there is convenience in keeping a communication route open dawns and a fort allows for northern access and egress. There appears to be a large card-shaped anomaly partially under the approach road from the roundabout and the entrance to Chesters that may be a temporary camp site. The author continues his research.

Take your time here; it has been heavy going, the feet deserve a rest.

Chesters Roman Fort
www.english-heritage.org.uk/daysout/properties/chesters-roman-fort-and-museum-hadrians-wall

The advantage of stopping at Chesters is that there is a convenient bus stop at the George Hotel.

There are also excellent B&Bs.

Greencarts B&B
www.accommodationinhexham.co.uk
Carraw B&B
www.carraw.co.uk

The author likes this village – it is alive. Unlike many villages, this one is fighting back against the tide of becoming merely a dormitory for folks that work in Newcastle-upon-Tyne and it has a very fascinating history. Ask the locals about the paper mill and its part in the Napoleonic Wars. Do use the shop, a community project that deserves your support.

Humshaugh Shop
www.humshaughshop.co.uk

And certainly pay a visit to:

The Crown Inn
Humshaugh
Hexham
Northumbria NE46 4AG
Tel: 01434 681 231

There might well be time for a stroll after some refreshment:

█ Humshaugh Walks

www.northumberlandnationalpark.org.uk/humshaughwalks.pdf

The walker has travelled a very reasonable 18km; a little easier than Day 3, but time is needed to enjoy Chesters and the author believes it to be imperative to get to know more than just the Wall, because there is so much more to see and it is all part of the greater picture. There is much ground to cover on Day 5 so get an early night. It is a long section ahead, so give the feet a treat – a good long soak!

For those wishing to plough on there is accommodation at www.hadrians-wall-bedandbreakfast.co.uk.

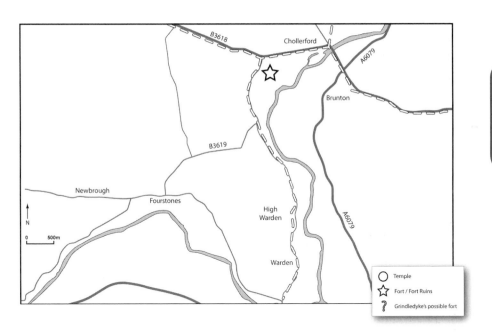

A DIVERSION

There is a building the author believes the walker should see; it is a short but useful expedition off the route and can be tackled today, should the walker wish.

Out of the gate of Chesters, turn left and at the end of the estate left again on to the B6319. Fortunately the walker is not on this for too long, dropping past the woodland down to the river. At Walwick Grange bear left on to the minor road and enjoy the view across the river; it becomes clear that the River Tyne has dug in hard on the walker's side of the valley over the last 2,000 years, leaving the old river bed high and dry. The road lifts itself up a little to keep out of the wet through Warden. Take a while to take the spot in sitting on a little hummock at a narrowing of the river. Warden is in two parts, Upper and Lower; the walker should head for Lower and NY913664.

Warden church is Saxon in origin and the tower in particular makes it very clear that it is something rather special. Look at the tower, the mass, the square

20 Tudor Rose detail at Warden Church

21 Warden Church. An exceptional structure in a magnificent setting

regular shape. Think turret. The builders of Warden had enough local remains of Roman structures to assimilate the designs; they could measure them and work out for themselves that if the Wall's structures were still standing up, if they copied them, they were not going to get it far wrong. The tower, save for the obvious extension on the top, looks remarkably right for the Wall; it is no accident. The author is aware that the size may not be quite right for some turrets, but it is the best we are to get regarding height and general form. The tower serves as a beacon of Rome's return; it is a confident expression of the power of the Church merged with local skill and historic design. The church contains another example of Roman material being reborn, the 'Warden man' – a gravestone made from a split Roman altar. In the churchyard is a seventh-century cross clearly providing a long pedigree for the site. Indeed, the author wonders if the altar may not have travelled too far from its place of origin. Warden church is a very interesting site, just above the floodplain, and there is a curious dip in the contour on its south-east side. The author wonders if small craft could, at certain times, make their way to Warden, providing a useful connection to Chesters. There appears to be a useful place to drag craft ashore, and an enclosure above the high-water line of the time. Across the way from the church, to the west, is a Norman motte castle (NY911665): www.pastscape.org.uk/hob.aspx?hob_id=18341&sort=4&search=all&criteria=WARDEN%20MOTTE&rational=q&recordsperpage=10.

The whole spot sits in a grand position slap bang on the confluence of the North and South Tyne. The site of the motte is private property and whilst the author would normally suggest politely asking permission to explore, time is against such forays. The Normans understood the significance, as had the Christian community that pre-dated their appearance. However, the importance of the whole spot cannot be over emphasised, which brings the author back to the altar. The site could also have a temple. This is a confluence of two rivers, an important spot: the river would crash the pebbles and boulders together and the gods would whisper. Enjoy the view and do make a goodly donation to the upkeep of this fascinating church.

The walker should consider some refreshment and it is close at hand; continue south along the lane and it brings the walker to the Boatside Inn.

▌Boatside Inn
www.theboatsideinn.com

Having thoroughly enjoyed the hospitality, the walker can cross the Tyne by a very substantial bridge. It has to be substantial – every previous attempt to bridge this spot has quickly failed. The present edifice has reliably stayed in place since 1903, so the author considers that it may well now have passed the test. Take the time to get a sense of the scale of this structure and its environment: note the flood works upstream; this delightful sparkling scene can be a grey thundering cauldron that will destroy everything in its path and regularly does. Turn left on to a footpath that will take you across to the railway and back into Hexham. If walking this route at night beware the foot crossing of the Newcastle and Carlisle railway. Take considerable care. You can continue towards Hexham without using the crossing, via the golf course and auction market. The station is the first left over the bridge.

1 Still with us after all these years. *Photographer Graeme Peacock*

2 Too neatly preserved – opinions please! *Photographer Graeme Peacock*

3 Banks beyond Birdoswald – a land to explore

4 Newcastle upon Tyne, a sunny Spring day

5 Arbeia Roman Fort, South Sheilds
– reconstructing the past

6 Something to look forward to –
near Housesteads. *Photographer
Graeme Peacock*

7 Man's works upon the land.
Photographer Graeme Peacock

8 Slyvian scene. *Photographer Graeme Peacock*

9 Housesteads Roman Fort from the Stanegate

10 The best advert you can get for walking the wall

11 Milecastle 39, Peel Crags. *Photographer Graeme Peacock*

12 Kings Stable Gilsland – life on the slope rather than the edge!

13 The Roman remains running parralel to the busy road. © *Countryside Agency. Photographer Graeme Peacock*

14 Warden, Cawfield

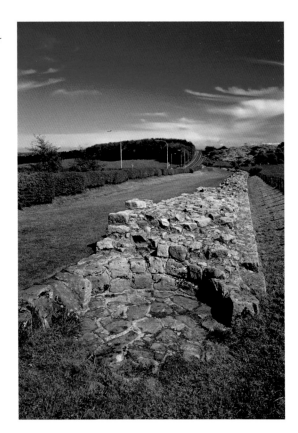

15 The northern face of the wall. Warden, Cawfield

16 The remains of Milecastle 39, near Steel Rigg, looking east from a ridge along the Hadrian's Wall Path. *Photographer Adam Cuerden*

17 Poltross Burn milecastle. *Photographer Simon Mill*

CHESTERS TO VINDOLANDA VIA HOUSESTEADS

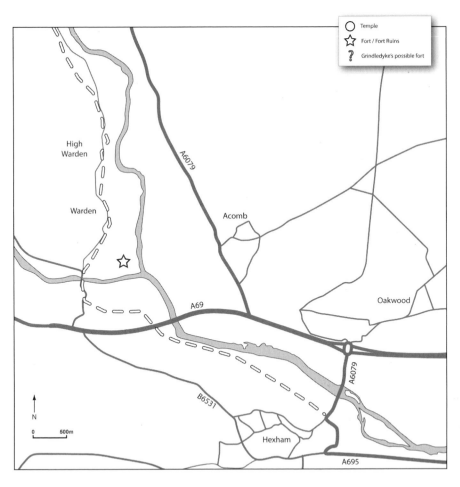

Legend:
- ○ Temple
- ☆ Fort / Fort Ruins
- ? Grindledyke's possible fort

High Warden

Warden

Acomb

Oakwood

A6079

A69

A6079

B6531

Hexham

A695

N

0   500m

- **Early start, 8.30 a.m. at the latest**
- **Boots necessary**

Using the bus stop opposite the George Hotel, head to Chesters.

Starting at the entrance to Chesters, head on by, along a good pavement; the road soon swings right to follow the Wall and vallum as it comes out of Chesters grounds. The National Trail takes a small deviation on the hill, follow it. The pavement vanishes and the way is better as indicated. However, it does mean that the walker misses a length of vallum deep and tangled with trees with a near-vertical edge to it. The author found this by accident, the vertical part that is – all in a day's work for an archaeologist.

The diversion soon brings you back on to the Wall itself, where nicely presented sections stand for all to see; this is jolly good stuff on the part of English Heritage and its supporters, as they previously were buried with gorse on top. The path is often busy with walkers; take the opportunity to stop and pass the time – information is always useful.

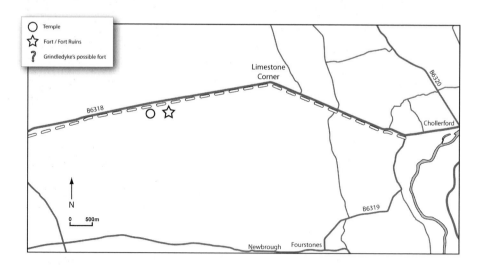

The way is straight until Limestone Corner, which is pretty obvious by its name, with a left turn. There is an impressive all-encompassing view here, with a Roman camp just across the way; from whence there would have been the sound of considerable debate sometime in AD 123.

'Well, I'm damned if I'm bothering to hack that out any further?'

The vallum is unfinished here. Just like the width of the Wall at Brunton, the actual instruction seems to have been interpreted to fit the situation or ignored. The strange thing is nobody else seemed bothered. The walker can find tool marks on the stones.

The turrets and milecastles are marked, which will keep some very happy indeed. Across the road the vallum is getting to be very impressive and the author has oft wondered if it deliberately imitates the landscape around it (the Whin Sill), folds of the earth caused by the plates stretching, leading to a series of sharp cliff ridges. The vallum becomes the most obvious feature until the windswept remains of Carrawburgh (Brocolita) Roman fort come into view.

DAY 5

22 Carrawburgh sits and waits for a trowel

23 Tribute: ancient religions not so forgotten, the *Mithraeum*

24 'Down tools lads' – a useless ditch feature that haunts academics to this day

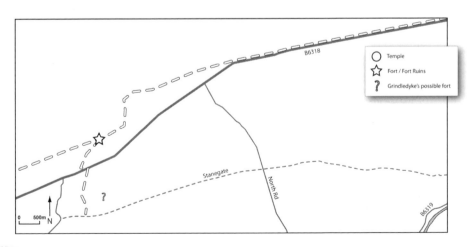

○	Temple
☆	Fort / Fort Ruins
?	Grindledyke's possible fort

The walker will wonder how this lonely forgotten spot could ever have been considered pleasant. The situation is gloriously empty; the view excellent, but there is a melancholy that is hard to explain. The fort is complete, in fact very complete, just beneath the unexcavated sod. The only part of the site understood fully is the Mithraeum and Coventnas Well. The walker can step inside the remains of the Mithraeum, but getting to the well is not easy as the ground is extremely boggy. The bathhouse is close to the same corner as the Mithraeum nearby (the Victorian excavation destroyed whole sections) and can just about be discerned by the dig waste mounds.

Carrawburgh offers an opportunity for further exploration of the Roman attitude towards place and how local deities played their part in a Roman frontier. The appearance of local gods shows that there was communication between the Romans and the local population. This points to a dialogue of trust – the locals were not likely to have revealed their gods to those they did not trust, as knowledge of local deities could be used as an important weapon by a hostile enemy. The gods tend to be those of place, and this involves the particular landscape in which they exist. The Romans are very aware of this; they need comfort and help – renewal of personal purpose. They have their 'home' gods, but any assistance, especially from a local god of place, is equally important. The local gods know the place better than anybody else; they keep the water sweet, the crops growing and the natives as friendly as possible. It costs nothing to show nodding allegiance to the local practices – it cannot do any harm and, possibly, a little good. As the author has said before, the Romans collected religions like stamps, but it is not just a collection, but a useful toolbox for getting through life and operating an empire.

The local gods are also a means of getting to know the landscape better; they are a talking point between native and Roman. The Romans acknowledging a local deity must be seen as acceptance; the fact the Romans changed the name a little didn't matter to the natives – they probably couldn't read, and even if they could it would be Latin and, therefore, the name would be of no original consequence as the Romanised name still allows for the deity's origins. If a dialogue is opened all sorts of information may flow regarding other tribes: the location of the ore for making offerings; the best place for sheep and cattle; the location of craftsmen; other sites for the deity. All very useful information which builds up an understanding of landscape, and a means of managing it; thus a spiritual need and a practical one are married.

The walker should consult this excellent work by Lindsay Allason-Jones BA MLitt: www.dur.ac.uk/resources/archaeological.services/research_training/hadrianswall_research_framework/project_documents/LifeSocietyOverview.pdf.

The author hopes that the walker will treat the gods kindly; they are still in the landscape. For the most part they are hidden away, but they are still doing the job they always did; we are no wiser for forgetting them. They play their part in managing the place, so we would be shrewd to protect them, if not give due adherence to them. For health, water and crops are what we all desire and a safe passing to another place when the others have faded away. If the walker imagines a thriving world of natives and Romans living and working along the Wall, the gods are the glue that holds the scene together.

Carrawburgh was constructed after the Wall; the vallum vanishes underneath it, which again undermines any obvious purpose. The fort is a handy halfway house between Housesteads and Chesters, close to a water source, which are naturally (to the Romans) associated with the gods. The inscriptions found so far at the site identify a mixed cavalry unit from the reign of Hadrian 1st Cohort of Tungri, probably stationed at Carrawburgh from their home base at Vindolanda for the purposes of building the spot. The longest resident military unit is the 1st Cohort of Batavians, occupying the spot for 190-odd years; this would explain the large civilian settlement.

Carrawburgh offers the author an opportunity to balance the walker's perceptions of life on the Wall. Wall building and military service is masculine; the very nature of the activity, the danger of the cut and thrust of combat, the comradeship of all the chaps down at the bathhouse, portray a man's world. It is, but not only: the balance is the women, often written into the background by historians; their part is equal, if not greater, in the day-to-day operation of the Wall.

Every fort has a *vicus*, a civilian settlement, a supporting unofficial substructure of the Roman army with ex-soldiers plying their skills and trades to the soldiers. There would be shops, blacksmiths, metalworkers, butchers, game dealers, bars and brothels, perhaps even a private bathhouse. Shrines and temples would flourish, especially if there was a local native god that, with a little Romanisation, would be added to their pantheon of deities. Holding this complex world together were women.

The author, having excavated Roman fort sites on and off since he was 8, has come to the conclusion that we have misinterpreted the day-to-day usage of the fort; that is to say, the commonly held view that troops live in forts. The author agrees that some men did, but that many lived out and attended to their duties much as our modern forces do today. Estimates of how many personnel forts along the Wall are built to hold are a joke. You probably could squeeze 1000 men in or 500, but not for very long; allowing for duties away from the fort or the shift system required to man its length, the idea of 500 men staying put in such a space is ludicrous. It simply doesn't work; one sneeze and the whole place would be out of action in a week.

The *vicus* was not only essential for amenities, but as a place for some of the men to live; especially as they had their wives and families along – which most if not all did. Whilst Roman soldiers were not officially allowed to marry, the regulation was widely disregarded and in AD 197 Emperor Severus lifted the ban completely; a significant date as at the time Severus was trying to get Britannia back into line after a serious revolt by Claudius Albinus, which appears to have been one of a series of placations to bring quell rebel forces.

Add to this the missing part of the jigsaw, the tented camps which leave no trace (or precious little) of their presence. From an archaeological perspective this is largely an unrecorded part of Roman military life and there is scant information about tented facilities anywhere along the Wall.

The weather may have been against such facilities, especially in winter, but they cannot be discounted as useful accommodation and they may open up a line of enquiry into troop movements and the changing seasons.

Through all this mud and mayhem, sunshine and shower, there would be women carrying on regardless and, in many cases, thriving. More of their exploits when the walker reaches Vindolanda.

The author is frustrated by this site; here is a largely unexcavated, very obvious Roman fort, with walls still standing, yet no attempt has been made to interpret it properly. The truth is he knows exactly why: money and, to some extent, willingness.

The author remembers a sherry party in Whitehall some years ago, when his ear picked up the following conversation, amongst the burbling small talk:

'We simply don't want to be having to run a seventy-odd mile linear theme park; somebody else can take it off our hands. It's simply too costly, a drain on our resources.'

'Give it to somebody else to worry about. Good idea. Make the Regional DAs pay for it. That's the way to go.'

Being the diplomatic sort the author has never mentioned this to a soul and never will. He does remember the canapés were jolly good; the rest was a bit of a blur.

But out of that conversation arose, some years later Hadrian's Wall Heritage Limited.

Yes, the Wall is a limited company with HM Government the beneficiary on behalf of the nation, and now controls the line of the Wall. It is an excellent

DAY 5

idea to have a single authority to deal with the day-to-day management and good luck to it. So sherry drinking does have interesting side effects.

If someone can bring people and jobs to a barren region and sustain that effort, all power to their elbows; except the world has changed. The RDAs (Regional Development Agencies), in particular One North East and the North West Development Agency are no more; the future is very unsure. How the Wall Company survives in these interesting times is uncertain; the Wall will survive and if the numbers that have trodden the route each paid £20 for the privilege, then many projects could be secured for a healthy future.

The major problem is an unwillingness to do anything in the way of major excavation, because that costs a great deal of money; better to spend it on baby-changing facilities, tea rooms, gift shops and inaccurate interpretation boards. Branding and marketing are important, they always have been – Hadrian was a great supporter of brand identity – but in this case the infrastructure simply is not there.

The population along the Wall, excluding Newcastle and Carlisle, has dropped by over 95 per cent, reaching 100 per cent depopulation in other areas. The excellent road system has never been replaced. If you then attract people to look at the remains of this land, it should come as no surprise to find it is extremely difficult to do so, which is off-putting for the day tripper – even more so when there are simply not enough local beds for the night to stay awhile longer and explore.

There are a few academics that deplore the fact the Wall has been opened up to the masses; it has provided them, over a good half century, a backdrop for an outdated view of Roman Britain. They see the Wall as being damaged, which to a degree it has been through erosion, but also because the cosy definitions have been blurred along with the stone. The Wall has been a backstop to theory; the inscription so far found along its length has provided the strands for a specific view. These views can be argued upon ad infinitum by the few.

What would happen if more turned up? It would crumble the comfortable towers of academia and puncture the balloons of those that have flown so high on mere whispers of second-hand wind. The fragility of theory meeting brutal fact never has a pleasant outcome.

The people want more of the Wall and the establishment do not. That is the end of the author's rant – he will have a short lie down in a dark pub and will recover anon.

Brocolita (Carrawburgh) must now be left behind; don't worry, it is used to it. This section to Housesteads is a joy if the weather is fine and hell if it is not. The vallum continues to impress with a regular formality – the walker should continue to wonder where it all went wrong back at Limestone corner. Filling it in at Brocolita does blur the necessity elsewhere somewhat, but to be fair there may well have been reasons to maintain the vallum elsewhere – if only as a water-drainage system. Some sections were over 3m deep and 6m wide, so Limestone Corner not being finished should tell us something, the only problem is we don't understand what.

The Wall is here very much into its high-profile role (cresting the edge of steep slopes, with dramatic cliff faces) making sure everyone can see just how good Roman engineering is and how fit and capable the Roman soldiers are. Walking this part of the Wall must have included steps and the only way to service this area would be by packhorse. There may well have been a role for the native tribes here, providing the packhorses and the carrier services. The Roman soldiers would have enough on their hands merely getting up and down this section.

There is erosion on this stretch, especially around the stiles.

> **!** Where repairs are being undertaken use the diversions.
> (This notice is not for the walker, for the author knows that they will abide by such directions; it is for the walker to gently remind others that do not.)

DAY 5

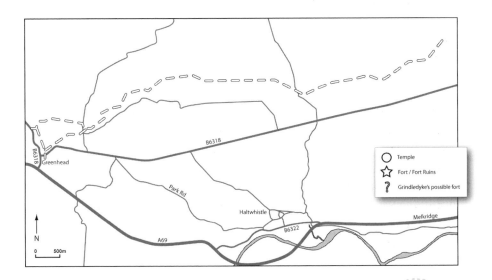

From Shield on the Wall, the Wall stays in view, apart from a missing bit before Sowing Shields Farm, and one does not need the author wittering about the view, milecastles, turrets and the lack of public houses. What is obvious is there must have been a disagreement between the Wall and vallum, for they go their separate ways, the vallum taking the more sensible path from its perspective, the Wall claiming the high ground in a very superior manner; they make up and are the best of friends by the time they reach close to Kings Hill. This seems to be a reasonable compromise in engineering terms, the vallum keeping in a straight line further back and not getting into a tizzy as it does at Limestone Corner.

Broomlee Lough provides a reminder of how wet the land to the north has become; the Roman aqueduct system along this section would have regulated the water flow, providing water for livestock, and the fort bathhouses alike, both requiring vast quantities of flowing water. The post-Roman era saw the system fall into disuse and the land returned to bog.

If the walker can work out where the Wall is in the missing bit, the author would be grateful to know. No doubt it was carted away to make an excellent barn somewhere – no digging mind!

Explore, investigate, theorise. Make a note, take a photograph, put the Wall back up, put the soldiers on duty – imagine. Take the time to see the past properly by taking the elements the walker has seen thus far to good use.

The Knag Burn gateway is an oddity: it allows access to the north and is not inside a fort. The Port Gate is the other example, although that may have been in a fort; it is unclear due to lack of research. However, the Knag Burn and Port Gate are so close to forts that full-scale invasion via them is unlikely. The Knag Burn has always wandered through this way; the gate came after the building of the Wall. The author considers the area on the north side to have been used for cow pasture; now a bog. There is indication of a drainage system and the burn appears to have been engineered in places. This is of great interest. The major source of water for Housesteads is on the north side of the Wall, making the site vulnerable.

You should be arriving at 2°19'42"W, 55°0'54"N. If not you are lost.

You should be at Housesteads (Vercovicium), and what a fort it is. Except of course it isn't here; well, it wasn't when Hadrian built his Wall, just a turret and a wall.

Housesteads is an English Heritage site, as is the entire Wall, but in this case it is operated by the National Trust.

> ## Housesteads
> www.english-heritage.org.uk/daysout/properties/housesteads-roman-fort-hadrians-wall
>
> www.nationaltrust.org.uk/main/w-hadrianswallandhousesteadsfort

The author will direct you to the latrines. This most important facility requires careful attention; firstly, it is built with the bread ovens next door, thus providing a nice warm atmosphere – especially useful in the winter. The walker will notice a channel round the latrine. It was once considered that this had running water in which the users dipped sponge on sticks for the purpose of wiping their backsides. It must have been a very good party for anyone to come up with that idea! The thought of every Roman soldier and citizen wandering around with their own sponge is bizarre; that and the fact that there would not be a piece of sponge left anywhere in the known world. Accidents with the stick don't need thinking about. The other factor is the fact that everyone is sitting together, very publicly.

What seems to be forgotten is that the remains are just that: the solid bits that cannot be ripped out – lead piping and woodwork, raised water troughs and partitioning, all of which would leave not one trace. The most important feature is the running water. Housesteads is unusual in that it has no water supply other than water troughs – there is no well; it is a dry site. This possibly explains why Hadrian's engineers didn't bother with it and popped down the hill to Vindolanda instead. There is water at Housesteads; the walker will have squelched through or over it: the Knag Burn, at the bottom of the hill. This served as the *vicus* and bathhouse supply.

This latrine would require a constant water supply. Either there was a constant supply via a wagon with barrels or there was a mechanical means of getting the water up to the fort. There are numerous water troughs within the fort – understandable, if it was short on water. But the Romans fully understood the need for fresh, flowing water, so here is a puzzle worthy of further research.

On Roman Poo

Barley was a major crop in Britain at the time of the construction of the Wall. The climate at the time allowed it to be grown in places that have since been beyond the boundary of favourable climatic conditions for the crop, though this is changing again. Faeces samples from the Wall forts have been analysed and wheat, rye, barley and oats have turned up along with bran, suggesting a healthy intake of bread, porridge and stews. The author is pretty well convinced that the presence of barley indicates beer making as well. Meat, fowl and game, along with fish and nuts are all recorded.

The local supply of honey and cheese would have helped sweeten and vary the recipes, along with herbs, all available local to the sites. There would have been the import of sauces; the Romans enjoyed a good well-rotted fish sauce, and shellfish would turn up in the most remote of spots, suggesting the military way saw fishmongers thrashing along with fresh deliveries on a daily basis.

At Housesteads the latrine's contents left the fort by stoned culverts, but were not wasted. The solid matter and the urine would have been divided by a settling tank at some point because the urine was valuable for curing leather. This settling tank would require management; all the content would find use on the land. Most faeces samples therefore could be from a period of decline when the management of the systems was haphazard or had stopped altogether.

The diet does suggest that Roman military personnel were regular, and a good quantity of olive oil consumed in the food would have eased things along very nicely.

In many ways the *vicus* is as important as the fort; there are clear remains of shops with accommodation at the rear and in one of these is a murder mystery to be solved. The *vicus* nearest the fort has been thoroughly excavated. The author urges you to find out more at www.pastscape.org.uk/hob.aspx?hob_id=15299&sort=4&search=all&criteria=Burghley%20House&rational=q&recordsperpage=10.

The author conducted research to the immediate south-east of the fort, on the land between the *vicus* and the road, and has noted large enclosures for another element of life on the Wall: the provision of meat (large quantities thereof, on a regular basis), wool and new horses. Wool was very important: the natural waterproofing of the wool provided the basis for a very useful piece of military kit, the hooded cloak (*cucullus*) – something to keep the winter blast out, but also to keep the soul within. There is an interesting cross over between religious belief and practical work wear that may be deemed to be part of a fetish within a religious context. Within the Housesteads museum is a stone relief, deemed by academics until recently as that of three women wearing tightly fastened cloaks. It is more likely to be three men. The cloaks act as a cover to their gender; however, from the breadth of the shoulder they look like thickset soldiers just about to go on patrol. The practical and the religious are blended into one, part of a Roman's everyday life.

The *vicus* is large; nothing unusual in that, all the forts have reasonable-sized *vici*, some very large. At Housesteads the presence of the enclosures suggest a regular herding of stock to the spot; this would attract traders and services but be it sheep, wool or even horse there would have to be some processing, shearing and slaughter areas and, in the case of horses, corals, stables and paddocks. If wool was being sheared en masse at Housesteads it may suggest it was a centre for weaving. It certainly had a water supply for processing, with the Knag Burn providing a constant supply, especially as it was canalled to the north of the Wall.

Housesteads and its environs should keep the walker busy for a while – on a sunny day it is a nice spot to have a picnic – but there is more to do. The walk now diverts from the National Trail and takes the footpath below the museum, towards the south-west, through the remarkable cultivation terraces. These are post-medieval, associated with lime burning, quarrying and lead prospecting, and appear to be well-worked plots, capable of growing potatoes, leeks, carrots and cabbages. All hearty stuff for the pot and, by the scale of the terraces, there was a fair-sized community living at Housesteads. It is a pity that no attempt has been made to do more to research and perhaps offer a restored working bit of terrace and one of the many ruined structures from this period. The walker will have noted the Chapel Hill between Housesteads and the road, which is peppered with an incredible mix of Roman and post-Roman domestic structures.

Beware the road, turn left and in a few paces cross and turn right; the Whin Sill will be providing a reasonable barrier, but the path makes for a clear track up and through it. The destination is just beyond East Grindledykes Farm. The path skirts the eastern edge of the farmyard and begins to descend the ridge. The fields to the walker's left proved to be of considerable interest to the author for several seasons; there is good reason to consider that there is a large temporary Roman camp under the sod, potentially more than one, sitting one upon the other. There are the remains of native roundhouses right on the northern edge of the Sill. The author would sit in the remains overlooking Housesteads and have his lunch, a most comfortable outlook. Excavation found the remains of more permanent structures in the area, including an apsidal building. The work was exploratory trial trenching and even with the assistance of the then leaseholder no further works could be undertaken for want of funds. Grindledykes remains, like Carrawburgh, for another day; at least it has been duly noted.

At the top of the slope at the entrance to the farm the walker should turn right; the Whin Sill provides an undulating walk and whole parts of the landscape vanish and then reappear. The bit in front is big enough to be seen from all directions and unsurprisingly has a settlement on it, and a potential

25 Author's anomaly, Grindledykes. Is this Hadrian's temporary camp site?

Roman signalling station. Closer to hand, the road, which is straight and level, is of equal interest: there is a very apparent ditch on the far side, over the Wall. It is a narrow-gauge railway line which carried lime, stone and coal down the Chainley Burn to Bardon Mill, and it will run parallel with the road to the junction, where it will pop underneath and reappear as a broken embankment heading down the valley. It is the remains of a line built to take materials from the pits and quarries to the east of Grindledykes.

The walker may wish to look back along the road they have just walked. It is straight and good; this is partially down to the National Coal Board, but they had assistance from the Romans; this is part of the Stanegate (Roman road), heading to Corbridge. In this very rural setting, coal, limestone and stone was mined and the whole remained profitable into the twentieth century.

There is an excellent walk into the Chainley Burn that gives the walker an idea of the industrial nature of the area. This site is operated by the friends, volunteers and supporters of Vindolanda and is not on the official Vindolanda website.

▌ Chainley Burn Walk
http://s9.zetaboards.com/We_Dig_Vindolanda/pages/walk1_chainley

If time allowed (which it really does not), the author would take the walker down the Stanegate; there are a myriad of adventures to be had along this particular length. The author remembers when he was working at East

26 Grindon Lough. The level would rise and fall with the pumping of water from the coal mines

Grindledykes the tenant farmer took him down to Grindon Lough, a wide expanse of water which was half dry due to a hot summer. The farmer wanted him to see the channels and pipes that allowed the lough to be used in the mining process; the remains of the foundations of a large pump house were viewed. This industrial archaeology, interesting in its own right, would have been enough, but what was also revealed was a sophisticated over-engineered series of stone channels heading north. One dropped into the ground and apparently re-emerged into the Beggars Bog and another headed for the Grindon Hill mill site. From the size of the stonework it was remarkably similar to the slabs used at the Knag Burn.

East Morwood, a little way down the way, straddles the Stanegate and appears to sit on an ancient site, worthy of further investigation. There is a Roman fort site, utterly forgotten, under Newbrough church and the road junction. The fort platform is very clear and appears to have been constructed to protect the river crossing.

The author may be persuaded to relate how one of the country's most eminent archaeologists in his early years in the profession surveyed the site, went to the pub (you see, it's not just the author), drank freely of the fine ale and managed to forget he ever recorded the site at all. He only remembered when he was reminded by the author many years later. But there again, the author might not decide to tell you all about it. These things are best forgotten.

If the walker ever feels inclined to wander this way again, and the author hopes they will, the Red Lion is a must. You may forget you were ever there.

Red Lion
www.redlionnewbrough.co.uk

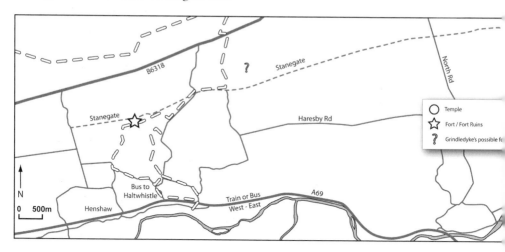

Closer to home, to the right at the junction, the well-preserved lime kilns lie in the dip; they are of considerable size, there being no shortage of raw material. Good interpretation signs show the process but do not tell of the human costs this process incurs; lime production rots the lungs and life expectancy for workers is not good.

However, Vindolanda awaits; around the bend and turn right, down the steep hill, past the car park and over the old level crossing, then left through an avenue of trees to Vindolanda.

Vindolanda
www.vindolanda.com

The author will leave most of the archaeology to the Vindolanda Trust to explain; this is because Vindolanda is the one site that is actively excavating and doing research. It is privately owned and funded by contribution, which the author hopes you will assist by not only paying the entry fee (buy a ticket for all sites – as long as you can use it on the following day, you will not get to the Roman Military Exhibition today) but a donation as well.

Notice that Vindolanda is hidden away. It is not on the Wall, but is part of its infrastructure. It pre-dates the Wall's construction, assists in its building and is the backbone of the military establishment. Probably Vindolanda had responsibility for regional matters, rather than solely the Wall; it certainly was the hub of the local postal service.

Vindolanda is an emerging story; there are at least two forts on top of each other and recent research has identified at least another one, all with complex histories. There are also unique native structures within Roman forts and the most wonderful discovery of all: the written word. A pile of bits of blackened wood found in a peaty ditch are the remains of small, fold-in-two writing tablets; each frame would have had a thin layer of wax within it on which a message could be made with a stylus. Though the wax is long gone, the scratches survived and when viewed under x-ray conditions, the life of the Wall came alive.

These scribblings – invitations, pleadings and day-to-day military instructions – bring the stone remains to life.

All power to the elbows of the Birley family and the Vindolanda Trust, which run the site. They have got on with the job and made ground-breaking discoveries that have reshaped our understanding of Roman life; unlike others, who have found every reason under the sun to do nothing. The author is very much in the 'do it' camp – up the revolution!

Women and their role in Wall life are well portrayed at Vindolanda, going some way to balance the military picture. The fact that there are major settlements alongside these forts and a thriving economy allows for women to play a part in the operation of the Wall in many ways. The elite female would be involved in behind-the-scenes political manoeuvring to assist her husband in his promotion; invitations to parties and felicitations to others that could assist; words in the right ears that in turn would mention the information at just the right moment either to good or ill effect. At the other end of the spectrum, there would be the women of the brothel and the slaves – generally exploited but surviving in the environment, and often their voices have survived as well as the elite's – not necessarily in tablet scratchings, but in devotional items.

The Wall would reverberate constantly with gossip: who's getting promoted; how much the price of oil has gone up and had they seen the state of the Prefect last Friday night – and that would just be the men!

The pottery finds at Vindolanda are considerable and assist in our understanding not only at Vindolanda, but elsewhere along the Wall; valuable in dating sites and understanding trade and the routes taken. There are accounts of bad roads in the winter around Vindolanda – pottery would have a very rough passage. Bathhouses needed oil for cleansing the body; oil for lamps; wine travelled in amphorae and was for the most part served in pots (save for the officer classes); there would be a need for basic vessel replacement as a result of accidental loss. Either the residents and troops made special provision every winter for the roads being closed or most forts had a kiln nearby.

See more at: www.dur.ac.uk/resources/archaeological.services/research_ training/hadrianswall_research_framework/project_documents/Pottery.pdf.

Late 2010 saw the excavation of a barrack block of the fort; a pit was found under the floor in which a girl's body was found, with hands apparently tied. This is clearly a case of murder; burials were never allowed in military sites – a spot suitably designated outside the fort would be the place for legitimate interments. A body buried in a pit (it is unclear to the author whether purposefully dug or not) would be a case of concealment and thus deeply disturbing to Roman attitudes to death and the dead, and a breaking of military code. We learn from the archaeology around the interment that it dates to the mid-third century, which quite possibly puts someone from the 4th Cohort of Gauls in the frame for the crime. The inscriptions found at Vindolanda identify a regular number of Belgae Gaulic legions passing through; an altar, of great size and weight, is proof of this:

I.O.M. Dolocheno Sulpicius Pu dens praef coh IIII Gall V. S. L. M.
'To Jupiter Best and Greatest of Doliche, Sulpicius Pudens, prefect of the Fourth Cohort of Gauls, fulfilled his vow gladly and deservedly'
(Prof A. Birley translation)

A body under the floor putrefies; the smell of rotting flesh is unmistakeable. Roman soldiers undoubtedly would have known the smell, a smell like no other. So how anyone expected to get away with it, indeed did get away with the crime, is quite remarkable. Possibly the building was temporarily out of use, the smell put down to blocked drains, which would no doubt keep someone busy trying to sort out. However, the whole incident poses considerable questions. The fact there is a child in the fort comes as no surprise; the author has already indicated that Roman forts, whilst officially under strict military control, were more domestic than anyone would probably like to admit. There would be slaves all over the place, freemen and no doubt women, girls and boys carrying out domestic tasks at the commander's official residence. We do not need to dwell on the exact nature of the crime, but whatever happened it undoubtedly needed to be covered up to prevent the truth coming out.

The author believes there might be some clues that may link a dead girl and an altar. Namely, the altar to Jupiter Dolichenus – this seems to be a last gasp for the god; by the mid-second century the cult of Mithras was more popular with the military. In typical Roman style, there had been a merging of place and gods, with Roman absorption of Commagene (present-day southern Turkey) into the Roman Empire. The gods came as part of the package and it was a reasonably popular choice with the soldiers and emperors alike; this was to ultimately backfire, as with any god or individual seen to be on the wrong side in a conflict, and by the AD 250s and the end of Severan dynasty, the god and his homeland had been ripped out of Roman control.

However, there would always have been rumours regarding religions of Commagene that some of them involved human sacrifice and, even worse, that of infants. There is a work (sometimes ascribed to Lucian) that described rites of one of the Baal religions of Commagene in detail; so the officers and men would have been aware that whilst Jupiter Dolichenus was not directly involved, he came from a region where such religious beliefs held some sway. The fact that the work, *The Syrian Goddess*, is deliberately ascribed to Lucian, born in the region, gives additional authenticity to the story. Lucian died around AD 180, but the explicit nature of this short work would through notoriety have still been readily brought to mind in the 250s.

The altar and the child's body were both found in the fort; altars don't normally turn up inside forts unless they have been dumped there during a demolition or scavenging phase. The idea of a shrine inside the fort, especially for a private rather than public deity requiring a close-knit membership, is very unusual indeed. If the altar is definitely contiguous, and there is no reason to think it is not, then it is indicative of a religion on the back foot and senior officer devotees who were holding on and ascribing allegiance to the god not only for themselves but for their legion as well – this would not have necessarily been seen in a good light by the men of the legion themselves. Nobody in the military or empire at large could have failed to notice that the Severan imperial line was on its last legs, and the Severans had been big devotees of Jupiter Dolichenus.

If the child is found to have been buried alive, it may well point to the one historic occasion when the Roman world was on the point of collapse: when Hannibal destroyed the legions and nearly brought the whole edifice of Rome down in 216 BC. So desperate were the Romans, they buried sacrificial victims alive in an attempt to restore the balance in their favour. This act was deemed, even at the time, so appalling that human sacrifice was seen as a point beyond which no Roman would go, and the Romans were not known for the squeamishness. The author wonders if at Vindolanda devotees of Jupiter Dolichenus, facing what they perceived to be the last days of the god, and with their personal positions within a Severan world about to implode, in their desperation took 'one step beyond' in an attempt to restore things to their favour. It wasn't worth the effort, or the loss of a young life. By AD 235 the god was gone and the old Severan order with it, thrown into the turmoil of the mid-third century; Mithras and the soldier emperors were triumphant. The body lay under the barrack floor where it had been placed, like the bodies beneath the paving of the Forum in Rome; everyone knowing where it was, but everyone equally too ashamed at their inability to stop the madness and do anything about it.

The other point to make is that altars give a false picture of adherence of units to gods; the officers are erecting altars to their personal deities and affixing the legion to them. Whilst the Romans were willing to allow a free-for-all in respect of belief, the affixing of a military unit to particular gods may have an effect, good, indifferent, potentially bad – especially if the god is out of favour. Whilst an annual dedication to the gods was standard practice, the officers risked ill feeling in the ranks if they did not take into account the popularity of particular gods. This included local deities. There are numerous inscriptions identifying spirits carrying out duties within the forts that are formally acknowledged; 'ignore such minor deities at your peril' seems to have been the order of the day – best to erect a stone, giving them due deference and thus keeping the troops happy. This may have promoted certain local gods to a greater status than they actually had in the wider world.

This is a theory, and the author quite readily accepts the fact he may be wrong; that is what theory is about – it offers questions as well as potential answers. If nothing else it provides a momentary chink of light into how the gods were present in everything and that the symbiotic relationship between the real and the ethereal could have life-changing consequences. The finding of the girl's body is an intriguing if disturbing insight into the dark side of Roman life; no doubt further research will reveal more details in the forthcoming years and Vindolanda's expertise in archaeological research will provide a full and precise account of the crime and victim's circumstance.

Vindolanda will absorb the walker. Why not join the Trust and book a course in practical archaeology?

TIME FOR PRACTICALITIES

The walker should be considering getting to a place of warmth and comfort for the night; there is local accommodation.

Accommodation

www.vindolanda.com/accommodation.html

The walker does not need to retrace their steps, but head out of the main entrance of Vindolanda, turn left and head down the hill. Keep straight down the hill, do not turn left. No footpath on much of this route; beware the traffic.

Henshaw of the A69 is the destination. There is a frequent bus service along the A69 either to Haltwhistle (far side), eight minutes, or Hexham, 23 minutes, from outside All Hallows church.

The walker has marched approximately 28km.

Just in case the walk down to Henshaw to catch the bus is too much:

Taxi Companies

Sproul Taxis
Tel: 01434 684 658
Turnbull
Tel: 01434 320 105

A DIVERSION

'The hill with two rivers' is a very rough translation of the name Haltwhistle. The town flourished by the fact there was no shortage of wool and water in the region; with the water supply operating powered hammers, fulling of the wool was possible, and dyeing and spinning along with it. Add to this a gradually improved east–west road system and the eighteenth century saw the town flourish, if with added noise and smell. Haltwhistle was actively involved in promoting a canal to improve its trade; this eventually became a promotion of a railway and a railway it got. However, the idea of exporting cloth worked against the town as the railway brought cheaper goods in.

Haltwhistle has five bastles (defensible farmhouses); these are 'centred' (the author does not apologise for the joke, which the armchair reader will not be able to see) around NY 708641 and a castle NY 712641, all of which are worth a second glance. The town is a good spot to explore and it has to be said that Haltwhistle is making a very good attempt at attracting Wall walkers to its delights. The considerable number of bastles in such a small area highlights the fact that Haltwhistle was prosperous in the days of dyeing and spinning; wool and the movement of sheep was an important and profitable trade, and the merchants had to be able to protect their goods against those irrepressible freelance entrepreneurs with added guns and pikes, the 'Reivers'. From the thirteenth to the seventeenth century, Haltwhistle was a honeypot with little in the way of outside help and a poor road system, so whilst relief was awaited, the thick doors and stone drops provided security from the raiders.

There are good shops for provisioning and a number of public houses in the area; the author has been known to undertake research in the area. There are excellent communications from Haltwhistle by train or bus to Newcastle and Carlisle.

The Black Bull, Market Square, is worth a second glance, or three.

DAY 6

HOUSESTEADS TO GILSLAND

- **Early start, no later than 8 a.m. at Haltwhistle station for the AD122 bus service to Housesteads**
- **If arriving from Hexham, no later than 8.50 a.m. at Hexham railway station for the AD122 bus service to Housesteads (check rail timetable for train times)**
- **Boots necessary**

The walker should alight at Housesteads and make their way up to the Wall; turn left and begin the most intensively walked part of the Wall. The author has walked this section both day and night and it is never really quiet; there is always some earnest walker pounding along or a charity event taking place with competitors strewn in wild profusion upon the landscape. Housesteads to Gilsland is the most eroded part of the Wall; it also has some steep slippery slopes and many an ankle has twisted itself here. Of all the sections it is the most dramatic because of its geography and nature, but for peace and tranquillity it is best at dawn or dusk, when the imagination can run riot. The past creeps, ghost like, into view; the walls arise and the shadows betray cloaked figures looking ever northwards.

Archaeologically this section isn't that stunning, which may upset some, for this is the best-preserved stretch. The Wall becomes a constant companion, but the eye

 The weather can make this a very hard crossing indeed. Rain or constant sunshine takes its toll. Good preparation is essential.

is drawn to the view north, taking the attention, which is oft the cause of a tumble. But enough of this apparent negativity; there is a long way to go, and is enough to keep the milecastle spotter happily occupied.

Life in a milecastle must have been one of continued shift changes; one half of the squad of eight to twelve men resting, cooking and messing while the other patrolled. Each milecastle would require provisioning, so there would be troops assigned from the forts to deliver oil, faggots for braziers, foodstuffs and the daily gossip. How long troops were stationed out at milecastles is hard to calculate, but one of the Vindolanda tablets is a request for more underwear and socks. Allowing for winter conditions and the difficulty in getting wool dry, and the classic 'stand up by themselves test' for underpants, probably two weeks; after which life in the milecastle would be unbearable for all concerned. The Romans had a good idea about the need for flowing water. Some milecastles present logistical difficulties, and supplies would need to have been delivered by barrel, suggesting a need for rationing at certain times.

The author thinks there was a double rota system: a squad would march out from the fort to the milecastle in the late afternoon to takeover for the night; the day squad would march back from the milecastle to the fort, with each squad breaking the day and night between them equally. This would mean that the milecastles were divided up equally regarding the forts along its route. It does suggest a considerable amount of daily movement and it is only the

27 'Okay, where's it gone? I'm going to close my eyes and I expect it back when I open them'

author's idea. He is open to other suggestions. Especially as the King's Stable milecastle has enough room for double barracks, suggesting the squad did a day and night shift; possibly because of the need to cover two bridges in a very short distance.

There would have been need for barrel stands, a set of woodworking tools for light repairs, and axes for timber spools. There would have been cooking equipment hanging up over the hearth stove, an area set aside for devotions to the gods, bunk beds and coat hooks by the doors for equipment and the all-important winter cloak.

The stonework of a milecastle gives us size and internal division. It, however, gives little away as to the likely large pile of logs by the entrance gate, probably with an awning, from which game would be hanging. There would probably be some oil jars, deliberately kept outside to prevent fires from engulfing the building. Undoubtedly there was a hitching post for horses, for when the officers turned up for an inspection, and possibly spare equipment such as a cartwheel. The walker can add to the list as they see fit.

Quarrying has destroyed a goodly and most dramatic corner of the Wall at Cawfields, but this does give the walker a chance to consider the vallum that has been somewhat overlooked as the elevated view attracts the walker's eye northward. The vallum, feeling unnoticed, puts on an excellent display; the fact is that it is completely and utterly useless, as any major force wouldn't attempt a full-scale attack on a cliff face, for this is the case along this 15km section, with notable exceptions where the Whin Sill has been eroded away, creating a need to plug possible intrusion points with additional turrets. Such points are obvious to defender and attacker alike.

DAY 6

28 Cawfields. Investigate – more than you think here

To the south of the vallum, at Hole Gap and Cawfields, are a number of Roman camps; in fact, the number indicated on the ordnance is a conservative number, there being several on top of each other. These appear to be construction camps, but were potentially sites to which troops could be deployed to in case of trouble, as an additional back-up for the Wall.

A number of Roman waterworks can be traced if the walker goes north of the Wall at this opposite, the ground is boggy so keep to the road. On the left there is a most impressive Roman camp; some of the aqueduct system may have been to keep this site dry.

Time for luncheon and there is but one excellent choice a very short distance to the south across the military road at the crossroads.

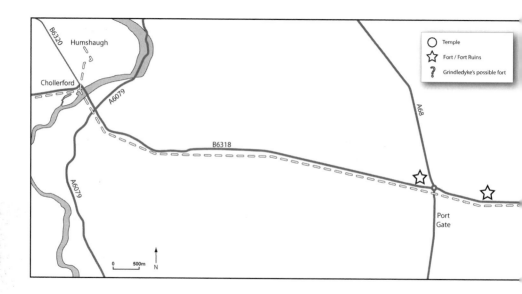

Milecastle Inn
www.milecastle-inn.co.uk
Tel: 01434 321372

Having had a good lunch it is time to move on, which normally will take some doing after a stop here.

Head back to the Wall – on the way have a good look to the left. The lumps and bumps are some serious Roman camps, semi-permanent with water supplies, suggesting they served initially as construction camps. There appear to be attached structures, potentially bathhouses and a *vicus* rather than a farmstead, the proximity to the military way and the relatively flat area allowing for horses and grazing – water into the camp might suggest re-use as stables?

There are over 50 camps along the Wall, though the exact number is not known – they are still turning up. So the walker has a chance of being part of history in finding one! See: www.dur.ac.uk/resources/archaeological.services/research_training/hadrianswall_research_framework/project_documents/Camps.pdf.

Next, head for NY704667.

Great Chester (Aesica) is one of the most fascinating forts anywhere on the Wall. It is an absolute one off; it conforms to the usual playing-card shape, somewhat obscured by the modern farmhouse. All tickety-boo on that front, until the archaeologists realised that the foundations for the Wall had been started at this location as broad wall, and then abandoned. The Wall, instead of incorporating the broad workings, finds new foundations immediately to the north of its unused broad ones, leaving the broad ones to be incorporated into the fort as part of its north wall.

Whoever gave the instructions to stop building a broad wall back at Brunton tower obviously didn't get the word to Aesica quick enough. The author can imagine the language in the bathhouse when the penny dropped. The other factor that is puzzling to all concerned is the four western ditches; as if an attack was likely on the flank. The southern side manages to interfere with the vallum, and yet again the vallum comes off worse in the encounter. There is no northern gate, the Wall being of a higher priority, and frankly there is nowhere for it to go, even if it had been built.

The fort seems to have been squeezed in. It may have been in charge of the water supplies in the area; it was certainly supplied by one, at over 9km in length. The *vicus* lies under the fields between the south-east side of the fort and the Milecastle Inn, around the temporary camps.

The turret numbers are in meltdown at this point. What joy.

Walltown Crags marks the beginning of the end for the most spectacular stretches of Whin Sill. A kilometre of Wall was happily quarried out here. The National Trail crosses the road here and turns right and then immediately left on to the line of the Wall. To visit Carvoran, turn left and head down the road and turn right; the entrance is clearly marked.

Excavation at Carvoran (Roman Magnis) uncovered a *modius*, a corn measure – a bronze bucket to weigh out the volume of corn to calculate taxes (*annona*) owed by farmers. It clearly indicates that there was a thriving large-scale agricultural network relatively close at hand, which is somewhat hard to believe considering the terrain in the area and the amount of waterlogged land; the author wonders if it ended its days as a bucket!

Carvoran seems to have suffered more than most; there is little to see, but the Roman Army Museum is certainly worth a visit. The fort site and *vicus* have been investigated at some depth and it's a shame that the site could not be brought back to life; it would add so much to Greenhead and possibly assist in getting the railway station on the Newcastle to Carlisle line reopened. The National Trail avoids Greenhead in regard to its route; the village deserves the walker's business.

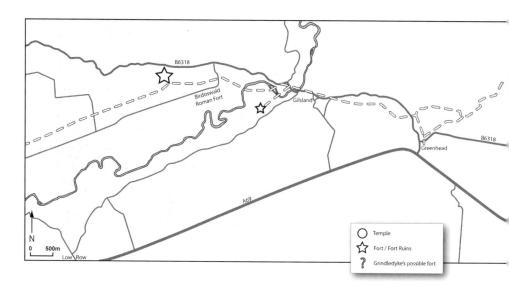

Greenhead Hotel
www.greenheadhotelandhostel.co.uk
Gilsland & Greenhead Food & Drink
www.hadrianswallvillages.org.uk/EatingOut.aspx

The walker has a choice at Carvoran, walk down the Wall to the bottom of the hill and then turn left for the village along the contour above the river side (note the direction of the flow), or still turn left and turn left again halfway down the Wall across the fields on a less well-used path; this does give the advantage of understanding the landscape and how the road (Stanegate), vallum, Roman service road, Wall and northern ditch worked, especially in relation to a river crossing. This path is close to the remains of the fort; it does descend at an angle and can be slippery.

There is a well-built footpath on its own course down the road.

Greenhead means the high ground at a watershed; in this case between the River Irthing and Tipalt Burn. A handy guide can be found at: www.nationaltrail.co.uk/hadrianswall/uploads/Greenhead05.pdf.

29 The Stanegate pre-dates the Wall and is still in daily use

Greenhead has a lot going for it and the head of two rivers may well have been very significant to the Romans and the natives alike. The author suggests a small diversion which will mean going along the path parallel to the river immediately across from the pub. This will take the walker to the river; cross here and have a look at the twelfth-century Thirlwall Castle, rebuilt of Wall stone in the fourteenth century. This is a strategic bridging point; it is possible the Roman Wall was converted to a bridge, but disrepair resulted in it being used as building material for the rebuilt castle.

Thirlwall Castle
www.northumberlandnationalpark.org.uk/understanding/historyarchae-ology/thirlwallcastle/thirlwallshorthistory.htm

The building has been restored. Included in the restoration is the vegetation growing on and in it; part of a joint project by English Heritage and English Nature.

The walker must retrace their steps from the castle, turn right and cross the railway line.

DAY 6

**Extreme care must be taken.
Look and listen both ways.
Do not linger.**

After crossing the railway, cross the road and follow the Pennine Way signs that will take the walker up the vallum, which is rising very steeply indeed; turn right onto the footpath that connects to the National Trail, which has walked along the road and missed the experience. Mind out for the odd golf ball.

The Wall and the vallum appear to take two separate paths here. The Wall keeps on a straight path. The author muses that it would have had an impressive crossing for the Wall, with a bridge section that would have had to accommodate the steepness of the climb to the western side. A small restored section of Wall can be viewed alongside the road, which cuts through it, showing that there have been considerable changes in this dip since the Wall and bridge were built and lost.

The author has thoroughly researched the area between the Irthing and the Tipalt – an uncomfortable experience even in drought conditions. The Pow Charney Burn seems to be the remnant of a large lake, which joins the Tipalt at the footbridge near the railway crossing. The best way to view the divide is by train; there is very little between the west and east routes and there does appear to be nothing but a bog, which if removed could tip the balance of the Irthing to an easterly direction. Whilst this sounds a fancy, it would be possible to control the flow in either direction and the Romans liked to master water, for agriculture and industrial processes. Only a theory on the part of the author, of course, but there is no possibility that the ever-eager Roman engineers would have missed the opportunity to get in and have a go.

The walker must dig in hard as the contours get closer. To the left and just discernible is the Stanegate making its way down to the river crossing and in the fields beyond are two substantial Roman camps; no doubt one is to protect the crossing, and the other to assist building the Wall and bridge.

It is time some serious archaeological research was done to identify the bridge site and how it worked, and in doing so assist the locals in attracting more visitors. For example, the author has a suspicion that the Wall and bridge incorporated a mill; the amount of water available would make it a sensible site and the finding of a *modius* nearby would make sense.

The vallum begins to lose interest at this point and keeps a little above, as the Wall delivers the walker into Gilsland. Again there is no railway station, which would assist in making Gilsland the destination for tourists it once was in the grand days of the eighteenth and nineteenth century, when the Gilsland Spa was at its height as a health resort. It still has a very pleasant hotel and the grounds down to the Irthing are an enchantment, full of mystery. It also demonstrates how a building can dominate the horizon; it certainly stands out against the land beyond.

Gilsland has a sense of ancient importance; it has a considerable history and is not one place but a combination of individual settlements, which comes as no surprise to the author. There is a clue in the landscape which all the pre-Roman tribes will have been aware of, a place which is still very distinctive today. The village now called Gilsland is an extremely important part of such a system because it is on a very important boundary: the place where sacred rivers divide and tribal boundaries meet and, with the natural rolling lie of the land, there is a natural temple mount and place of meeting. The probable extent of Selgovae boundary towards the east is the River Irthing, where it meets the Poltross Burn; this provides a southern boundary with the Carvetii. The Votandi, the equivalent tribe to the east of the Selgovae, has a southern boundary of the Tyne. All the major tribal players have reason to see Gilsland as significant; in particular the Carvetii, for the River Irthing, which feeds into the Eden that in turn feeds into the Solway, is their northern boundary. The Votandi, with the eastern bank of the Irthing and the watershed to the east, flowing into the Tipalt Burn (and then the Tyne), have an east–west and a southern boundary with the Brigantes.

Time for a good rest.

The Samson Inn and the Bridge in are worth a visit.

DAY 6

Samson Inn
www.samsoninngilsland.co.uk

Bridge Inn
Gilsland
CA8 7BE
Tel: 01697 747 343

Turn left after the pub, head through the old station yard and follow the footpath signs; the way descends quickly into a steep, rather dark gorge, with the railway bridge bearing down from above. Across the bridge and then up

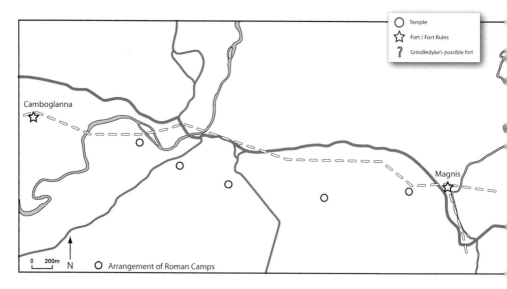

Temple
Fort / Fort Ruins
Grindledyke's possible fort

Camboglanna

Magnis

0   200m   N   ○ Arrangement of Roman Camps

30 Gilsland camps or forts

the other side the King's Stable is reached or, to be precise, a milecastle, built on the gradient making life for its occupants one long uphill or downhill battle. The author feels this particular milecastle posting can never have been popular, especially in winter – unless the soldiers enjoyed sledging. This is one of only two double-barracked milecastles on the Wall.

There is a set of Roman bridge abutments and side walls hereabouts, with a 70ft wooden crossing of the Poltross Burn excavated in the late nineteenth century; this is reported as the crossing for the Stanegate. The author has had difficulty finding this site; perhaps the walker can assist?

Greenhead and Gilsland offer another glimpse into the relationship between the Romans and the natives; the spring lies to the north of the Wall and there is no attempt to enclose the area to prevent use of it by the natives. The Romans can access the spring from the fort at Magnis or Banna (Birdoswald), on the northern side. Considering the ability of the Romans in heavy civil engineering, there is an acceptance of the existing arrangements and the gods are rightly left well alone.

The twenty-first-century walker is unlikely to be distressed by seeing a buzzard fly over an oak tree with a mouse in its claws, or a red fox with a white hare, the sun crossed by crows or the sound of stones turned over by the bubbling stream. Everything in the world had a meaning to the Romans and an appropriate action to counter any ill effects.

In the twenty-first century the residents of Gilsland, indeed of any property along the Wall, live with ever-present 'genie of the trowel' – archaeological investigation is usually required before any works involving holes in the ground can take place. From an archaeological perspective this is the only way the past gets to be examined on the Wall; there being no money for any other way.

An example of a typical archaeological assessment: http://ads.ahds.ac.uk/ catalogue/adsdata/oasis_reports/northpen3/ahds/dissemination/pdf/ northpen3-20826_1.pdf.

The day's walk ends here.

There is good accommodation in Gilsland and the walker has managed a very respectable 18km.

Accommodation
www.willowford.co.uk
www.tantallonhouse.co.uk
www.brooksidevilla.com
www.hillonthewall.co.uk

DAY 6

DAY 7

GILSLAND TO WALTON

- **Start by 9 a.m. at the latest to get the most out of the day**
- **Boots necessary**

From the Samson Inn the walker should proceed under the railway bridge and walk through the village, taking the left-hand turn in the centre of the village for Upper Denton. Go up the hill and the walker will clearly see a fine section of Wall. The house with a tree growing out of it, which the chickens seem to love no end, should also be noted. The walker will no doubt as to why a national monument has a chicken scrape on it. The chickens seem to enjoy their imperial home so that is all that really matters. Take the right-hand turn on to the trail at this point.

The walker will note that back over their shoulder across the railway is steep-sided rising ground, on top of which is a Roman construction camp; at least that is what we currently believe it is. As with Greenhead, the southern side of the valley is sprinkled with such camps. They all seem to be next to natural springs which suggests that such spots could be useful for drinking and washing water, and equally damp and unappealing places in the winter. These camps have been recorded. They also appear to be quite permanent, including waterworks to get the excess away, but possibly to supply bathhouses. The author has suspicions that there was one near Throp, quite close to the railway line, and readily available to the men at the King's Stable milecastle. See more at www.dur.ac.uk/resources/archaeological.services/research_training/hadrianswall_research_framework/project_documents/Camps.pdf.

There is another Wall construction camp (for that is what the author has decided to call them) on the river side of the railway, sitting immediately above the Willowford bridge site, and it suggests a direct link because of its location. This makes the author wonder how difficult it was to manage this location in Roman times; how very different it was and how the Romans engineered their way out of the valley bottom, but also how they coped with the river gods. It is very difficult for us in the twenty-first century to comprehend, but let us examine the evidence: the other camps are high above at this point, out of the damp, or out of the damp and out of the influence of the gods as well? The walker will have noticed that Gilsland sits between natural geological hillocks. Historically Gilsland was a series of independent homesteads. Is it possible that each of these held religious significance and thus power; power that had to be placated, managed, subsumed and integrated. This was not just a civil-engineering job; this was a religious experience. This is not the only spot along the Wall where religion is part of the package, but it is possibly the most dominant site because of the setting and the natural springs in the area. Academics, historians, archaeologists and walkers alike tend to forget that the landscape is alive to the Romans and natives in a way we are now oblivious to.

A fast descent on to a river bottom. It is clear that the river once occupied all of Willowford; the clean lines of the bridge built to take the National Trail over the River Irthing are in view. More importantly, the remains of the Roman bridge, especially its abutments, can be seen. Three bridges have occupied the site, two of wood. The third bridge was able to withstand the torrents slightly more successfully, built wholly of stone. The Irthing, angry at having its fun spoilt and to get its own back, promptly moved its course, leaving the bridge high and dry.

The author has wondered around in a dizzy haze (not unusual after a good lunch) looking for any sign of a temple or shrine in the immediate area; river gods must have abounded hereabouts. The Gilsland Spa attracted its custom from the two springs bubbling into the Irthing; the Romans would thus have seen the river as sacred – doubly so with two springs. Bubbles of a chalybeate and sulphur emerging from a cliff face into the waters would be a notable sign of the presence of the gods. However, the author's search continues.

The River Irthing is the county boundary between Northumberland and Cumbria, and the Millennium Bridge now crosses the gap.

When the walker reaches the middle of the bridge they are in Cumbria and it is all downhill from there on, except for the bits that go up.

There now follows a repeat of the steep ascent that was required at Greenhead, to allow for the Wall to gain the westerly bank of the river; the National Trail does a quick zigzag to gain the height. The vallum re-emerges to the left and the Wall to the right; however, next to the vallum is the remains of a well-built bank. This is the Turf Wall, remains of which will continue all the way to Bowness-on-Solway and beyond.

DAY 7

31 Looking back to Gilsland

A comprehensive synopsis is available here: www.dur.ac.uk/resources/
archaeological.services/research_training/hadrianswall_research_framework/
project_documents/TurfWall.pdf.

The section of turf wall seems to have been abandoned along this section
because of the possibility of the whole structure toppling down the slope; the
idea of putting a stone wall so close to such a drop would not be lost on the
Roman engineers.

Particular attention should be given to location NY 620664.

Look out for the good-luck sign. A very popular symbol that can
occasionally be found in stone walls and buildings off the Wall, which assists in
tracking down exactly where and when it went.

This part of the National Trail is immaculately kept, like a lawn, the
sheep playing their part. Birdoswald is soon met; the Wall's keeping at a very
respectable height throughout the journey.

The playing-card fort survives; there is an excellent interpretation of the site
and the chance for a cuppa. Enjoy the visit.

32 Birdoswald Fort. Gates facing Gilsland

Birdoswald (Banna)

www.yha.org.uk/find-accommodation/northumberland-north-pennines/
hostels/birdoswald/index.aspx
www.english-heritage.org.uk/daysout/properties/birdoswald-roman-fort-
hadrians-wall

Birdoswald (Banna) has a huge civilian settlement to the south and west, only restricted by the sheer cliff face down to the river; part of the southern *vicus* is in the river, slipping away in the night and taking the residents with it. This possibly explains why the *vicus* spread west, away from the edge. Several thousand people lived outside the fort, the Wall supporting them and they in turn supporting it in a symbiotic relationship – all reliant upon the continuing presence of the military machine to service.

There is an excellent series of photographs of the excavation undertaken in 2009 on the cemetery site by Newcastle University that the walker should have a look at. Excellent work.

Banna pre-dated the Wall and appears to be part of the earlier pseudo-frontier or segregation line (author's theory), which was in place by AD 112. More details at: www.english-heritage.org.uk/professional/research/archaeology/birdoswald.

North of the Wall from Birdoswald, a Roman road runs 11km out to Bewcastle (Fanum Cocidi), believed to have been constructed around the same time that the turf wall was going up; but the author suspects that further work as to the earliest foundation needs to considered. The fort is not of the usual square or playing-card shape, but six sided. The fort is believed to be named after the local deity Cocidius and, in typical Roman style, he was added to the Roman pantheon.

DEO SANCTO COCIDIO ANNIVS VICTOR CENTVR LEGIONIS E
'To the divine god Cocidius, Annius Victor, centurion of the legions, recalled to service'

Cocidius turns up along the Wall in many spots, but also within the north in general. He appears to be a hunter based on two tiny silver plaques of rough but clear work excavated at Bewcastle, suggestive that the devotee had produced them rather than pay for a craftsmen, the effort being part of the vow to the god.

A six-sided fort is an odd one, save for the landscape. It is a series of rolling hills and an offensive force could easily take advantage of the cover; the fort covers every angle possible. The author also considers that the presence of a bathhouse within the fort and the likely *domus* may point to an enclosed shrine complex that doubles as a fortification. Enclosure of sacred spaces is a feature of many religions and peoples, the Romans being no exception. Cocidius started life as a native god which became part of the Roman pantheon; in this case the Romans physically surrounded the site, which contrasts with the bubbling waters of the river gods at Gilsland where they are nominally outside the cordon of Roman control.

Whilst Bewcastle is physically detached from the Wall, it is protected by signal towers and the author considers archaeological field work may reveal additional military structures on either side as appropriate to the landscape to enhance control further.

The walker could consider a visit if they can afford another day, as it is a 22km round trip from Birdoswald. Check the time of the last AD 122 before attempting it – Bewcastle is a long way from anywhere! The going is by way of tarmac; the exact Roman route of the road is unclear in places, the ordnance being a tad too direct.

Above: 33 Bewcastle
Castle. A delightful
rural residence in need
of some attention

Right: 34 Bewcastle
Church & Cross

DAY 7

It is time to leave Birdoswald; with the knowledge that like Housesteads it never completely went out of use and has never been forgotten – if something is useful in Cumbria it survives. If not it is taken to pieces and reused, reused and reused again; nothing is wasted. It is a marked feature of Cumbria that archaeological sites are often absolutely clean of every possible reusable item.

Just to the west of Birdoswald a botanical survey took place in the excavated vallum bottom: http://services.english-heritage.org.uk/ResearchReportsPdfs/099_2010WEB.pdf.

It is good to report that many of the plants and trees from the Roman era have survived on the same spot: oak, alder, bramble and hazelnut.

The National Trail commands and directs the walker westward, the vallum, Wall and Roman military road in unison striding out along the ridge (although there are sections where the vallum decides to do its own thing). This is a very satisfying stretch with good walking; no serious grade and easy path, or road should the walker wish, although this not a good idea when the traffic is busy. Regular turrets well interpreted and all remains in harmony until the askew tower at Pike Hill is met; built at an angle to the Wall and causing the connection to stagger. This tower is a signal station for communication, probably with Bewcastle. It pre-dates the Wall's construction and, as demolition would cause problems with communications, it was built into the system.

The tiny hamlet of Banks (aptly named) is reached when the present road moves away from the vallum, the Wall taking a slightly higher contour to ease the construction. The hillside is a series of humps and bumps, and the cottages take what little level ground they can. Living with a multiple vallum, for this is the case here, does not come easy!

The walker will be aware of the excellent use of location on this stretch. However, whilst it is dramatic to the walker, it was even more dramatic when in use; the walker has seen it, for the most part, from the bottom. Plus the walker is viewing the Wall from east to west, but the Roman soldiers would have spent most of their time looking north, with east to west meaning home, bath, beer and bed; so whilst there is much in common with today, the understanding, the perception of landscape is different. The door of the next turret or milecastle is more important than staring on to cattle pastures and farmsteads. The walker sees a pleasant way ahead, relaxed upon a holiday and personal quest; the slopes, thrills and spills along the way colour the view. It is not routine, it is not a slog in all weathers; for the Romans, whilst there would be comradely company and the odd laugh, the view was one of monotonous waiting for something or someone to happen out beyond the Wall.

Above: 35 The steep descent to Dovecote Bridge

Right: 36 On Dovecote Bridge one early Spring morn

DAY 7

Turn left at:

355409 E
564508 N

Down the hill to Lanercost Priory, which seems to have taken just the odd stone from the Wall in its construction; the Augustan canons certainly had a good eye for a location. Very grand tearooms and a shop are available. The priory is worthy of investigation, but mind the time. The 122AD bus stops outside the remains of the gatehouse.

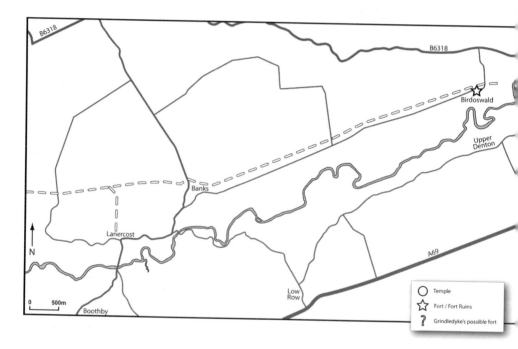

▌Lanercost Priory
▌www.lanercostpriory.org.uk

There is a B&B just down the way, by the old abbey bridge.

▌Abbey Bridge B&B
▌www.abbeybridge.co.uk

To keep to the Wall you must return the way you have come; it is steeper going back up but worth it for the view. There is no doubt the canons took the stone away from the Wall via this route. The author wonders if they used an incline of timbers and sleds rather than wheeled carts on this grade; there appears to be a cutting on the right of the track. At turret 54a (number crunchers tick another one off) the walker will be glad to know that things got very confused for the Roman engineers building the turf wall, not one but two different alignments suggesting not only construction but repair of the original structure before complete rebuilding in stone. Considering the position it is amazing that no stone was used in the first place to give a better platform, which raises some questions as to the permanency of the turf wall. In these locations five years and the whole structure would give way, especially after snow and a typical Cumbrian rainy summer.

Historians and archaeologists have concluded that the Wall's construction started in the east. What caused the western stretch to be of turf could be expediency to get the frontier made as per imperial orders. Hadrian undoubtedly wanted the hemming in of the empire to be a physical thing; so it is possible that all involved could report 'mission accomplished' (whilst turret 54a quietly slipped down the bank). Add a shortage of good stone without having to import it from west Cumbria, which would take time and effort

37 The Wall emerging – on the way to Walton

and would apply from Bowness-on-Solway to Stanwix, then the walker has a reason to use turf. Alternatively, the frontier may well have been considered temporary beyond Gilsland. The Rivers Irthing and Eden could be of religious importance to Roman and native alike; enclosing it may have been seen as a short-term policy – a case of 'look what we can do if you don't co-operate'. As the author has already noted, the spring bubbling up is on the native side of the frontier, as if deliberately not preventing access – a diplomatic move perhaps? The turf wall wouldn't hold any army up for long and is frankly not that impressive to a native race with sophisticated timber enclosures; it merely acts as an indicator of possibilities to come. In a few words, the author hasn't the faintest idea, nor does anyone else yet. Archaeology may solve the problem and the author suspects the answer will be found elsewhere in the empire – an imperial edict or an inscription – we shall see.

Turn left at Haytongate or you will fall off the other side of the crag. Instead, the walker will descend nearly as quickly towards the footbridge over the Burtholme beck and ascend the other side. Allowing for the switchback, it is more sedate than those at Carrawburgh and Greenhead.

The walker should now head for NY 5392 6427. It is possible that the walker will not be able to see this feature because it is a farm; however, the vallum is likewise worthy of diversion.

The author admits this inscription is now barley visible, but decided that it was worthy of attention, because it is oft overlooked. It should read:

CIVITATE CATVVELLAVNORVM TOSSODIO
'Civitas Catuvellauni rebuilt' [dated to AD 369]

Further details are available at: www.pastscape.org/hob.aspx?hob_id=12816.

The diversion has no doubt been of benefit if only to give the dog in the nearby farmhouse some fun. But it does show that pride in workmanship is a constant throughout the use of the Wall. The fact the inscription has probably just travelled from the top of the track, where it will have been hacked out along with the rest of the Wall and deposited in the building, gives a continued sense of place. The stone is now higher than it would have been when it was set up in the first place; the eyes that viewed it when new saw it in a different context: pride and thankfulness for a job well done.

This is why the author has taken you to a farm on a hillside in Cumbria. The Catuvellauni are a native British tribe, busy doing remedial repair work on the Wall and thriving within the Roman system. In this case doing their bit to continue the Roman control of Britain, which was under some internal and external strain at the time. The Catuvellauni, more at home in their native area around St Albans, brought their wives and families with them and they in turn intermarried with other units on the Wall. A gravestone survives at South Shields with the inscription, 'Regina the wife of Barates', a Syrian soldier. The walker will have noticed this tombstone when visiting Arbeia; it is an evocation of love and Roman domesticity. Regina sits in a wicker chair with all her precious things in a box: jewellery, love letters (it matters not); the image binds Wall, native, Roman and empire into one whole and the worn inscription on a byre is part of that chain – strands of history apparently tenuous but strong enough to evoke emotion and understanding down through the centuries.

The vallum is very obvious here and is determined not to vanish, deciding to go off on its own and taking a completely different line, down the grade to the River King Water, from that of the Wall. The reality is there simply is no room for it to keep on the same line as the Wall, which again calls into question the reason for its existence. The descent from Howgill towards Low Wall sees the Wall quite prominent under the bank with a hedge on top; there is a very good chance it survives in its covered state. The farmers, seeing that the stone was not of good quality, realised that they to keep the boundary, they should cover it up; it is a story that is to be repeated shortly.

The modern bridge over the King Water appears and the walker is immediately aware of the need for quite a substantial Roman bridge; there was. On the far side the remains of the Wall approach to the bridge can be viewed or, to be precise, the earth mound protecting them, just as the farmers had done with theirs many years before. The local sandstone vanishes with the wind, so soft that the Romans must have had a constant replacement programme on this section. The bridge supports must have been a constant headache, unless they were of imported stone, and because of that durability they have long since vanished for reuse. The interpretation board provides a good idea of the structure. The vallum doesn't want to play and meets the King Water River's flow further south, avoiding the steep grade and keeping away from the village of Walton.

The Centurion Inn, Walton, is a great pub and more importantly it's on top of a milecastle. The author has done much research here and considers that there is more than just a milecastle at this location. The Wall takes a south-westerly turn at the milecastle. The Roman Wall surveyors used the position to get the direction along the crag tops towards Birdoswald.

The Walton milecastle could also act as signal station, additional protection for the two guard towers at the bridge, but the author also considers that there may have been a formal and suitably imposing gate nearby, allowing for the route to Bewcastle.

The Centurion Inn & Fell View Restaurant
Walton
Brampton
Cumbria CA8 2DH
Tel: 0169 772 438
Mob: 07976 810 369

From Walton on, the Wall and its line takes on a very different feel; for starters, the Wall completely vanishes. The National Trail provides the route, otherwise it would require a considerable amount of detective work. Very little visible evidence is on offer to keep the spirits of the walker up.

B&B in Walton
Walton High Rigg Farm
Walton
Brampton
Cumbria CA8 2AZ
Tel: 0169 772 117

Walking along field edges with hedges, the idea of a Wall or vallum soon slips away; this becomes a country stroll. Nothing wrong with that, but there is a sense of loss in the air.

Turn off the National Trail at Sandysike Farm and the vallum reappears and points the walker at Castlesteads, or where it should be.

Castlesteads (possibly Bana) is not available to the walker to view, it having been completely robbed out, or at least that is what we are led to believe. The grand house to its north-west contains some of the stone. The author considers it still worthy of attention, but considering how many other sites deserve attention it will be a good while before it is opened up for a proper going over.

View from footpath:

54 57 48.62 N
02 45 27.42 W

Castlesteads is not attached to the Wall itself, standing some way back, which is why the author believes there is a gate through the Wall at Walton, making up for the lack of one at Castlesteads. The *vicus* here was even larger than that at Birdoswald. The author has made a study of the land to the south-east, between the fort and the River Irthing. So the fort may be lost, but the civilian settlement remains – excavation of same would be jolly useful!

The walker should proceed along the footpath to the point where it meets the busy A6071, then turn left; the road is a dangerous place so be extremely careful on this section, including Irthing Bridge. Turn right on to a short section of the Stanegate; just before Crooked Holme turn left on to the footpath to Brampton old church. Bear right before rising up the slope and head diagonally across the slope.

This peninsula above the river is in fact a Roman fort; Brampton old church lies snugly within it.

The fort platform is very clear and the remains of the old church are worth a second look. There are interpretation boards to assist, but the reality is we don't actually know much about this site; it has never been excavated, which is understandable as this is a graveyard.

38 Brampton Old Church – a sense of history

The author remembers working on a dig with his father many years ago (in an age when a pint of beer costed 28p); the task was to find the course of a Roman road passing through suburban London. Father vanished to the pub with the sextant; two hours later the happy gravedigger wandered happily through the tombstones putting a chalk mark on the most difficult graves to dig and the direction of the road was proved without the need for any excavation. Those were the days.

It is thought that this fort was abandoned on the building of the Wall. If an attempt was made on the *vicus* that lies in the fields to the south this might be proved beyond doubt – or not, as the case may be. Speculation and theory have their place, but the trowel upon physical evidence proves the day. As for landscape, this fort is very well placed above the river, which is encroaching slowly against the soft earth face to the north-west when in flood; the tangle of willow not acting as any defence.

The walker can now head along Old Church Lane into Brampton; refreshment is probably required and there is no shortage of places to find it. The Shoulder of Mutton is but one of many excellent establishments, but

39 Line of the fort wall, Brampton Old Church

there is a need, for once, not to linger too long as good light may assist on the next stretch.

Walkers may note that the author has wandered off on one his diversions without warning. Life is full of surprises – all will be revealed.

Proceed to the south-west end of town and take the footpath from Elmfield towards Capontree Hill; beware the very busy A689. Keep on the old road (the new one keeps letting you know it is there) until you reach Low Gelt Bridge. Turn left along the left-hand side of the bridge; proceed up the river and you are in the Roman quarries for building the Wall. This is a magical place, but good light does help.

This is the site of the Written Rocks of Gelt, Roman inscriptions left behind by the soldiers. Do not expect to see them as they are not readily accessible; time (as is its wont) has also done its best to wipe them away. However, they are recorded. The Written Rocks of Gelt are not forgotten; the people of Brampton enjoy the spot, but few Wall walkers discover the place, so take your time to explore.

North side of river
IX X
'VEX LIEG II ΛVG OF APR… SVB AGRICOLA OPTIONE
APRO ET MAXIMO CONSVLIBVS OFICINA MERCATI
MERCATIVS FERNI'
N I S IIV III
AVIDI
IVLIN
IVL PECVLIARIS VEXILATIO LEG XX V V
EPPIVS M

Pigeon Crag
ARA FECIT IIVSTVS
LEGIONE SEXS ET
ET AMIO

Even without an understanding of Latin, the Roman numerals are the important factors. The legions have left their mark; the constant factor throughout the Wall is a desire to have the effort remembered as 'publicly' as possible, written so high that the 'public' could only be the gods, each layer of rock being hacked away in steps beneath it.

Let us examine the longest inscription in some depth:

VEX. LEG II AVG SV AGRICOLA APRO ET MAXIMO CONSVLIBVS
OFFICINA MERCATI

Which, when you expand, should read:

VEXIELATIO LEGIONIS SECUNDAE OB VIRTUTEM APPELLATAE
SUB AGRICOLA OPTIONE APRO ET MAXIMO CONSULIBUS
OFICINA MERCATIUS FERNI

And now in English:

Vexillation of second Legion (Augusta) under Agricola, Workplace of Mercatius.

Which dates this to AD 207 by the naming of Aper and Maximus as consuls. This falls within the imperial reign of Septimus Severus and his son Caracalla (from AD 198). Severus had come to power courtesy of the Pannonian legions in AD 190, who themselves served on the Wall. In this case the second legion Augusta had only quite recently been brought back into the Roman fold, having sided with Clodius Albinus in 196, who had decided he wanted the top job. Back in AD 122 the same legion had built the first stone wall, as the inscription at milecastle 38 identifies the legion. The quarry was thus busy on refurbishment of the Wall system against any attack from the tribes to the north.

It is possible that these and other dated inscriptions were the reason for Bede and others to believe the Wall dated from Severus, not Hadrian. The number of inscriptions and the work undertaken would certainly provide the spurious date of inception. It does bring home to the walker that any part Hadrian's Wall is much altered and replaced.

The river and the rock faces can be dark, forbidding places, but the scene is much enlightened by sculpture, wildlife trails, and the place of cries and sweat is now more often associated with the giggle of children enjoying the adventure. It is a casual portal to a different place, not lost on the Romans. As far as the author is aware no archaeological work has ever been undertaken around the entrance to the quarry to find the work camp. There are several potential sites, including the fields to left and right of the A689.

Return to Brampton by turning back at Middle Gelt Bridge; it is a pity there is no inn here. The railway viaduct is impressive above.

This is the end of a different sort of day: a few surprises and 11km of Wall completed, with plenty more kilometres on diversion.

Head into Brampton for the night or alternatively head to Carlisle.

Rail services from Brampton station (originally Brampton junction – indicating a reasonable walk along the track bed from the town station) give the walker access to the Newcastle to Carlisle line, offering reasonably frequent services. Bus services are also excellent from Brampton market square.

The walker travelled, with expeditions, a decent 25km today.

Travel information (train & bus)
www.nationalrail.co.uk
http://jplanner.travelinenortheast.info

DAY 8

WALTON TO CARLISLE

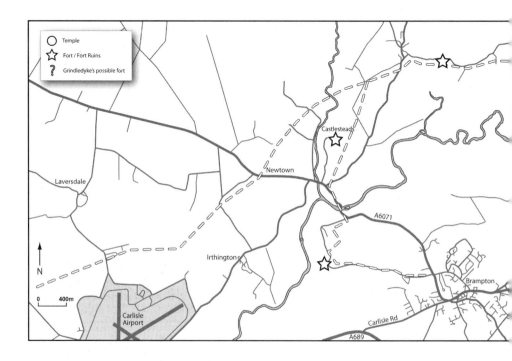

- **Start at 9 a.m. at the latest**
- **Boots for country, and soft shoes for town walking**
- **Terrain: Some muddy bits along the way!**

The walk continues from the Milecastle Inn at Walton; the fastest way to get to the pub is by taxi from Brampton. Otherwise, the walk is the reverse of the one to Castlesteads the day before.

▌Brampton Cars
▌*Tel:* 0169 773 386

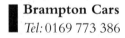

The walk is as the day before, except that this time at Sandysike the walker should go straight on along the National Trail, which begins a long, slow curve to the south-west. This is a very good march; the walker should carry plenty of provisions, especially liquids. It is easy walking all the way to the A6071 which should be crossed with the usual caution, though the idea of a Wall is far from the walker's mind by now. The errant vallum has vanished completely from the landscape, only to reappear, at least archaeologically, by the time Newtown is reached. Interestingly, the vallum is described now as 'Ditch'.

Carlisle airport is the dominating feature of the landscape and its presence only goes to emphasise that the walk is now on the flat; the heights of Limestone Corner and Walltown Crags are a mere memory. The Stanegate crosses the runway halfway down its length in complete ignorance of it presence. The Wall had been recorded by the Ministry of Works before the airfield was built and duly took the course into account.

40 On the wall, Bleatran Farm to Walby

DAY 8

The author is truly tantalised by the section between Bleatarn Farm and the junction with Wall Head Farm, mostly because of the nature around the Wall; as the land is not intensively farmed or improved and the Wall is so very close to the surface. Part of him wants this section exposed, the other, the practical side, quite rightly believes it is better under the sod, but it is a section of hidden Wall in considerable contrast to the rest of the way to Carlisle.

The walk becomes a ramble along a country lane, a byway, half forgotten; the idea of the Wall only remains in names such as 'Old Wall', 'Wall Head' and the 'Walbys' – the Wall's exact position was found at Walby Hall.

Whilst the author fully agrees, indeed fervently is in favour of private enterprise and supports the farmers, it would be nice to think that a World Heritage site might be acknowledged at Walby Farm Park. The Wall is the boundary of the car park. It is utterly forgotten and, like all other remains on this section, is ignored for the present needs of the infernal combustion engine. It is a disgrace that such an important part of all our past is being forgotten and the situation needs sorting out – the walker knows what to do.

Walby Hall
http://ads.ahds.ac.uk/catalogue/search/fr.cfm?rcn=EHNMR-1432966

The Ditch vanishes to be replaced by the title Roman Military Way, with the walker walking on the Roman Wall itself, or site thereof, throughout this section. There is a choice ahead. The walker can decide to divert to Crosby-on-Eden via the National Trail, but the author imagines by now the walker will make their own mind up; you never know, there maybe something new to see.

At NY4560 lies not one but three, if not four, temporary Roman camps; these sites close to the Wall are likely to be involved in construction or renewal, as elsewhere (Gilsland). However, some of these construction camps are useful and well-drained stopping places, continued in use because of their location.

These temporary facilities, just behind the Wall, re-enforce the fact that the region was an extremely busy one. Every time a legion moved a vast baggage train would follow: equipment, general military provisions and the 'followers'. Whilst troops could move quite quickly, they still needed an overnight billet and it made sense to have the basic open area ready for them to camp on.

Add to this the fact that everyone needed to have a means of daily provisions, plus the ability to find supplemental luxuries – troops had a daily ration, everyone else had to make their own arrangements, though in reality the soldiers had to make provision for their partners, wives and siblings. This leads the author to conclude that there was a well-established series of settlements along the Roman military way providing all the services required, filling in the gaps between the major forts.

Allowing for carrying a goodly load on the back and walking, or oxen pulling equipment trains, the speed of transfer would not have been great. One particular element that needed more provisions than any other was the cavalry: rest, fodder and water, with a good deal of space.

Thus some of the larger camp sites became focal points for civilian travellers to head for as dusk settled in. They would have been busy, noisy places; more a case of safety from the night than a good night's sleep. Such brief usage would only have left the merest of signs behind: the odd lost coin, brooch, horse fitting. This transitory effect, hardly bruising the landscape, is hard to trace, but the reality of such movements make them a practical necessity. There would have been the wayside equivalents of Little Chef, Travel Lodges and Toby Inns – all of which, being wooden buildings, have completely vanished.

These particular sites, overlaying each other, have been viewed from the air; they contain a series of pits, possibly for rubbish burial or potentially a multitude of temporary latrines.

For those that have stayed with the Wall, do not fear – beyond the last 'Walby' the Ditch, vallum and the course of the Wall can be discerned to the right. If the (weather is dry), just before the walker takes the footpath to Eden Grove and to the left, Low Crosby, Crosby-on-Eden via crossing of the A689; which is very dangerous.

It does appear that when the National Trail along the Wall meets private land in Cumbria, it does its very best to go round it rather than straight through, allowing for sensible privacy to the landowner.

However, such a diversion does allow the walker a chance of a pint and Crosby-on-Eden does have refreshments to ease the walker's thirst.

The Stag Inn
Low Crosby
Crosby-on-Eden
Cumbria CA6 4QN
Tel: 01228 573 795

DAY 8

A public house is always a good place to ponder and consider before venturing on. Crosby-on-Eden to the east is the site, though not obvious, of a palisaded Neolithic enclosure. There are two further Roman camps; again these appear to be sites in very regular if short-term use.

The author allows for this diversion not simply for the pub, though that would be enough, but even he has to admit defeat in being able to keep the walker to the Wall route. The Wall access rights and the practicality of where it has survived means that the National Trail and the author's route have to allow for a pretty big compromise at this point; that and a footbridge over the M6. The National Trail does its best and keeps the walker in the countryside as long as possible. The author is slightly less bothered about countryside; buildings are just as interesting if the landscape beneath can be discerned. However, the National Trail also allows bicycles at this point as well, which the author has some difficulty with – especially as no cyclist seems to have enough money left after buying their machines to afford a bell.

The walker may need a little help understanding that they have been traversing a site worthy of the United Nations Educational, Scientific and Cultural Organisation (UNESCO). Hadrian's Wall is now designated under 'Frontiers of the Roman Empire', which puts it into its proper context – part of a much bigger picture. The author would like to travel the entire Roman frontier, which probably has not been attempted since the fourth century – it'd make for a good few guide books and jolly good television; any takers out there in TV Land?

▌UNESCO Listing

www.unesco.org

A question that does require some serious consideration by the walker (and everyone else) is this:

Why are milecastle 9, 10, 14, 63, 69, 70, 71, 76 and 78 in such a state?

The author may not think much of an imposed numbering system, but he does care about the state of the archaeology of the Wall. Should a World Heritage site be under regular or intermittent ploughing? This is the case with the Wall: agricultural activity continues at thirteen locations. Is it not time that this was brought to an end? The UK Government is (rightly) the first to complain when someone on the planet is disregarding their heritage, yet at home we continue to do just that – we ignore the fact that we really should take better care of the Wall and we open ourselves up for derision by others. The author does understand the difficulties this may cause farmers – farmers have a difficult enough time as it is – but we are the all the custodians of this treasure and it deserves better care. Of course, money is the problem and the maintenance of what is currently on display, let alone additional sites, would terrify English Heritage and whatever body replaces it is hardly likely to see this as a priority. The author hopes the walker has an opinion and will act accordingly.

Just an aside: the milecastles under the plough are subject to 'a regular review' – the last occasion was September 2000.

The National Trail provides a very pleasant view and by pure co-incidence the trail is on the earlier tribal boundary, as the Neolithic camp would suggest. This gives the author reason to mention the tribes, the native inhabitants of the region which don't get much of a mention along the Wall; they seem to have been brush stroked out of the picture (other than comments regarding the Wall coming under attack) which does nobody any good, because there is plenty of archaeological material on their settlements and history and they are part of the whole Wall picture. The Romans certainly didn't build the Wall without input from others and there is no reason to consider this was a straightforward Roman master, native, slave relationship.

The walker should keep with the National Trail, the scenery is better than the hectic A689, especially through Linstock. Linstock Castle NY42895848 is worth a second glance, built as a bishop's palace in the twelfth century and the sandstone appears to have come from a handy pre-cut quarry site, the Wall. The first construct was, as per normal for this lawless region, a tower house, with walls 2m thick. The walker should stroll on through Linstock and over the M6, a noisy invasive place which prompts even the author to march away from it as quickly as possible.

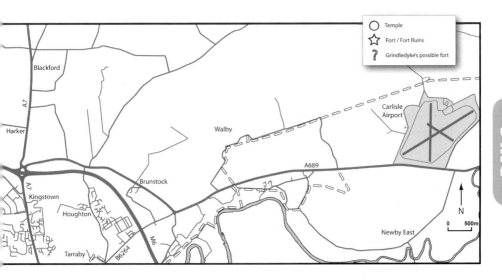

At Rickerby there is an opportunity to break free from the National Trail. At the far end of the village the walker should take the right-hand footpath by the Brunstock Bec, which takes the walker back on themselves towards Whiteclose gate; straight through the estate on to the main road, walk back out of town (right) a short way and cross the B6264 and next to the pub turn left.

Near Boot Inn
Tarraby
CA3 0JA
Tel: 01228 540 100

Head into Tarraby, which is a rather hidden away spot, and turn left on to the footpath; now you are back on the Wall itself. Considering this is the approach to a city, this is a very rural stretch. If using an OS map, the walker should note the ground to the south-west of Wall Knowe; for those not using an OS map, locate 545430.72N, 025550.00W along the footpath. It is slap bang in the middle of what is described as a parade ground. Now the author has a theory about Roman parade grounds, especially those in the north, anywhere near the Wall. As far as he is concerned they are not parade grounds; that is to say, you could parade men or cavalry, perfectly good idea and no doubt they were very useful for the purpose, but they are very much more likely to be for tented troops. Moving legions from place to place would have been a logistical nightmare and such sites would have been extremely useful. This part of the Stanwix site is not covered in buildings and has been investigated: a clay platform, 0.5m deep, which had covered pre-existing agricultural features and some earlier structures – some very useful digging.

The walker should be able to find the outline of Stanwix (Uxelodunum) Roman fort; the last few days will have provided more than enough practice.

As with Benwell there is little to see, other than a restored section; the English Heritage detailed description is useful to follow.

Stanwix is the foremost fort in the area, surpassing that at Carlisle. Its position and gateway to the north via its northern gate made it a major administrative centre and Carlisle a more provincial establishment responsible for the route to Bowness and beyond.

The position in the landscape allowed Stanwix to act as a signalling station to other forts and, with cavalry, could respond to any emergency quickly. In many respects this 'rapid-response unit' could be seen as a return to the Trajanic system that didn't require a Wall at all.

The Sixth and Twentieth Legions were responsible for the construction of the fort and it was garrisoned in its later days (fourth and fifth centuries) by the Ala Petriana, the one and only thousand-strong cavalry unit in Britannia, based on the Wall.

Such a unit would not have been cheap to keep in post. A 455kg horse eats 7kg of fresh fodder per day and drinks 68l of water. The author leaves the walker to do the calculation; allowing for other units having some horses, the Wall would be hard pushed to find enough fodder in the winter and grazing in the summer on its doorstep. It probably wasn't practical to keep more than one cavalry legion in a single location. This may explain the position of the cavalry unit, on an excellent communication route supplied from the agricultural belt around Old Carlisle (Maglona) and the nearest harbour at Kirkbride.

The walker should continue past the University of Cumbria buildings, and then turn left out to the Brampton road, where they should turn right, in preparation of heading down into the water meadows on which Carlisle sits on the edge.

The walker should now proceed into Carlisle proper and the descent into the town is a welcome relief on the feet. Note the amount of descent, which is a clear indication that Stanwix is the superior site in respect of the Wall and Carlisle is secondary, protecting a river crossing. The road is very busy, but the way for the pedestrian is broad and safe; it's just the fumes that will do the damage. Fortunately Carlisle is to have a new bypass to move the infernal combustion engine further away. Bear right at the large roundabout unless you are heading for the Lowther Arms, then head roughly straight on. On to Lowther Street for refreshments, methinks!

A DIVERSION

For those wishing to attempt to work out the actual river crossing from the northern perspective, cross the Brampton Roan, Stanwix road junction heading west, and turn on to Cavendish Terrace, past the cricket ground and to NY39735678, which is most likely the site of a milecastle on the edge of the escarpment before the drop to the river. Further understanding of how the Romans tackled this difficult river is yet to be fully understood. Only the Romans would have a milecastle right next to the military installation, which would incorporate a tower at each end.

BACK TO THE CITY

The walker should head back and enjoy the city.

Tullie House Museum is a must visit, but can be tackled the following morning if you're arriving late in the afternoon. To understand Roman Carlisle and the Border City in general, there is no better spot. By the time this publication is at the presses, Tullie House Museum will be a trust; please support the cause.

█ Tullie House Musem
█ www.tulliehouse.co.uk

The city is largely pedestrianised and offers all services.

█ Tourist Information
█ www.visitcumbria.com

As for public houses, the author offers his personal favourite:

│ The Howard Arms
│ Lowther St
│ Carlisle
│ Cumbria CA3 8ED
│ *Tel:* 08712 238 000

There are more, but as far as the author is concerned this is the best. It also is close to the point that the walker arrives in Carlisle. A Victorian pub with a listed exterior, easy to find by its green brickwork, the interior is a welcoming town pub. It has a horseshoe central bar with rooms adjoining still intact. There is somewhere for everyone to enjoy a pint; the author has always found it welcoming – the locals are friendly and the ale is well kept.

As for dining out, the author leaves it to the taste of the walker; there is no shortage. He does spend a lot of time in a subterranean Italian near the museum; you can always leave him a glass of something should you so wish. He enjoys the fact that he can sit in one of the booths and muse that he is at about the right level of the Roman town. That the hustle and bustle, noise and smells of Roman Carlisle are all around him as he sits in his comfortable time machine sipping a decent red. It's a tough life being an archaeologist!

The author will speak frankly: there is a sense of relief arriving at Carlisle, even when, like any city, there is good belt of suburbia to walk through.

The National Trail keeps the walker off the Wall because it is prettier by the river; legitimate to a degree, but it does detract from the purpose of actually experiencing the Wall. Importantly, the complete absence of evidence breaks the cohesion of the journey. The author deliberately started this journey of adventure in the east so by the time the section beyond Walton was reached, the walker would be able to use their skills learnt to detect whatever tenuous trace there was to their advantage.

Better to start with actual and then go to the theoretical, rather than try the opposite.

The fact that the Wall has gone comes as no surprise. Quality building material is always going to be attractive; we all would do the same in another age – it is not the practical reuse, it is the sense of abandonment and preferring not to remember.

When the Wall was being rediscovered and the way along it was being signposted, the route from Walton to Carlisle lost its signs on a regular basis, from being deliberately cut up. Whilst this is a modern reaction to the imposition of an administrative frontier, it indicates a deeper mood. Cumbria makes the most of its landscape, because it attracts tourism and keeps the staggering economy afloat; heritage plays its part and Hadrian's Wall is seen as a considerable bonus to that machinery. The walker will have noted an airfield (it would have been hard to miss it) and Carlisle airport is a modern gateway to Cumbria, the equivalent of the Port Gate; there is a public divide as to how much this airport should be used. It is seen by some as an invasion; by others as the way forward. Just as the Wall was seen when it cut through territory; it offered advantages at a cost.

41 Carlisle arches that lead to much needed sustenance

DAY 8

The author recommends a quiet night and a few pints at the north end of the city. Carlisle is a survivor; it has been walked through more times than it would like to remember. The border city is a turnstile of history. It has suffered, but it has also thrived, being the first or last administrative centre before Scotland on the west side of Britain. This created a rich merchant class and evidence of this has survived around the cathedral. The coming of the railway and the industrial age likewise saw a provincial boom in the mid to late nineteenth century. It brought expansion with typical Victorian bravado and unbridled confidence: mills, market hall, magnificent (if now woe-begone) railway station, parks and churches. A microcosm of Britain at the outer fringe and it is this distance and fringe that, on the one hand, gives it a certain air; certainly not charm, but more a sense of purpose – a place that gets on with life. It has, for the most part, kept within itself, not moving too much of its retail centre out. It has adapted to the changing fortunes, as it has always done, and it is of a human scale, no more than a large town anywhere other than Cumbria, where it is big. There is a divide: Newcastle-upon-Tyne is definitely the more powerful partner, attracting more inward investment and, by sheer scale, it has made sure it gets it. Carlisle makes the most of what it gets and does its very best to use what it has to good effect. The city is beginning to promote itself properly as a tourist destination with justification because of its history and remains.

The walker has trudged a very respectable 20km today allowing for some wanderings.

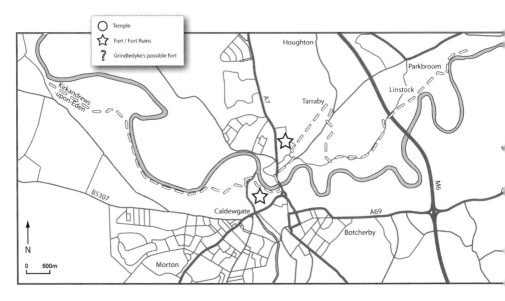

DAY 9

CARLISLE TO BURGH BY SANDS

- **Start at 9.30 a.m.**
- **Soft walking shoes for town walking**
- **Boots for the countryside**

 Public transport is sparse, west of Carlisle. Plan ahead.

The English Heritage website (www.english-heritage.org.uk) provides an excellent resource for understanding the native settlements along the Roman frontier; it will assist in the walker's better understanding of the wider landscape and how the land was exploited before and during the Roman period.

Welcome to the Border City, Carlisle (Luguvalium); a border courtesy of the River Eden and the expanse to the west of the Solway. This was an important crossing point long before the Romans were on the scene; indeed, it was a capital of a local leader which the Romans, for probable diplomatic reasons, incorporated into the name of the spot. The first Roman occupation appears to be *Legio IX Hispana* during the campaigns of Quintus Petilius Cerialis in AD 72 – the chap who did all the work before Agricola turned up and is credited with it by his father-in-law Tacitus. By AD 78 there is a hefty timber fort under Tullie House, the dual carriageway and the green by the castle.

Some archaeologists have suggested that Carlisle is the capital of the Carvetii tribe, a sub-tribe of the Brigantes, who held sway over the north up to the Wall region. The Carvetii occupied the top third of Cumbria; two other tribes

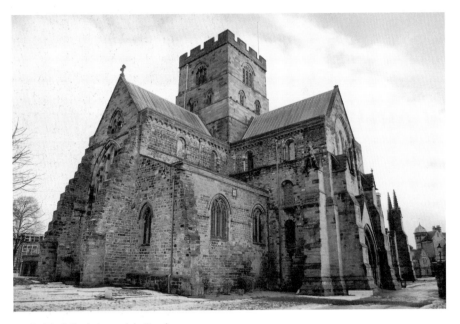

42 Carlisle Cathedral – much battered

are described, one of which is 'the sheep folk', which seems appropriate. The author disagrees with the theory on the ground that there is a very large native settlement at south of the River Derwent at Papcastle, which seems a more likely spot, not being on a border. Borders do tend to be subject to attack and having one's administration so exposed is not a good idea. That aside, Carlisle acts as a very good point for taxation: cross the River Eden and pay up is the order of the day.

Interestingly, post-Rome, Carlisle never proved very good at stopping anyone invading; possibly because the approach from the north is from a high point and the locals were border people so likely to be related to those trying to invade. Considering the castle's size, it does not have the most victorious history. The cathedral, worth a visit, next to Tullie House, shows the results of the lack of protection offered; it was partially demolished by them.

Hadrian's plans don't really include the Carlisle establishment: Stanwix is in ascendancy and it is much better placed and, importantly, it is on the northern bank of the Eden, not the southern. Here we see an important piece of military physiology, gaining the high ground, and also indicative of actual Roman control north of Carlisle; the first really steep grade in the local landscape and the Wall is up it, commanding attention. The Romans have the

43 Detail of the Tullie House Museum, Carlisle

sophisticated civil-engineering skills and the organisation to carry out the work. Carlisle, whilst a busy civil settlement, is not the biggest player along the Wall; this appears, based on geophysical research, to be Birdoswald to the east and Maryport to the west.

A must for the walker is Tullie House; make it first thing today.

Allow a couple of hours for Tullie House then proceed through the underpass by the northern exit of the museum; this will bring you out by the massive grandeur of the castle keep.

▌Carlisle Castle
www.english-heritage.org.uk/daysout/properties/carlisle-castle

Turn right along the footpath and then left down to the small car park and head north-east towards the river; take the first left, with the path running along the river heading north-west. This is roughly the Wall line. The author uses the word 'roughly' as the river has moved and the exactness of where the bridge crossed is a tad unsure; especially as there may over time been more than one and at different locations. There is evidence that the Romans made considerable efforts to control the river by building up the banks of both the Caldew and Eden with infill. This appears to have been more to do with the need for space rather than a genuine defence project, as Carlisle was a busy spot.

The author conducted some theoretical experiments in Carlisle, courtesy of his troupe of mature students attending a weekend archaeology course in the city. All were local residents and they were able to offer well-thought-out formulas for the Wall crossing the Eden and provided some extremely useful information previously unrecorded. This is a classic case of the need for continuing Wall research, which some of them are currently undertaking on their own initiative. Local knowledge and input, as ever, proved invaluable in archaeological advancement.

There is a pile (the best way to describe it) of stone that has at one time held a bridge up offered up for display, although the word 'display' is a generous one.

To the left there is a metal bridge heading for a sports facility over the River

Boots would be a good idea from here on!

Caldew; make your way over the bridge and then to the edge of the railway line to the left. Mind out for the footballs and the odd glances.

Right on the field boundary a stone will be found: Hadrian's Wall. Look through to the railway line, the main Euston to Glasgow route, and another stone will be seen sitting proud right between the up and down road. The course is suitably recorded as Hadrian's Wall, and how many millions of travellers have passed over it and not had the faintest knowledge it is there!

The walker should then try to fill the gap, both in history and time, and how much things have changed. The one factor that has been a constant presence is the river, the ever-changing river – a difficult thing to cope with, especially for a bridge and a stone wall. The very steep cliffs on the opposite side, the river plain and the edge of which being roughly the castle mound. Plus, as the walker will have noticed, an additional river crossing of the River Caldew to take into account; whilst much has been done here, there is more to do and understand.

To continue along the Wall, the walker should take the footpath at the edge of the playing field where it meets the Caldew and the railway; this sometimes floods under the railway bridge so take care. Turn right and then turn left, then right again; this will take you over the course of the Wall and down to the river. Turn left and you are on a rather damp National Trail. The Wall stays above to the left, continuing along the contour above the river. The railway bridge, sadly unused, gives the walker the scale of the structure needed to cope with the river and roughly the height above the flow required. Carlisle floods very dramatically and there is no reason to believe that it was any different in Hadrian's time.

Just after a footpath bears off to the left, up into the trading estate, the vallum re-emerges from under Carlisle. It may not be very obvious, but it is there. Nearly as quickly, the National Trail bears, with the river, off to the right and heads to Grinsdale.

44 Carlisle Cathedral detail

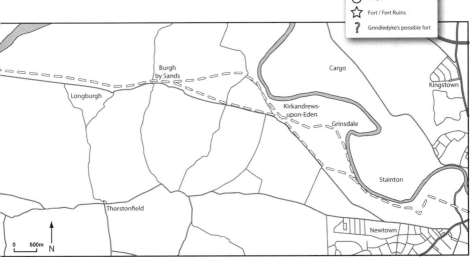

DAY 9

It is time for a little research:

NY 362570

The Nowtler Hill camp can only be seen as crop marks south-west of Grinsdale, so a good drought is needed to see them at all. NY 362570 is trapezoidal; the unusual shape makes the author consider the occupants might well have gone on to Bewcastle to prepare works there; they obviously had an eye for defence based on the particular landscape around them. There is an earlier camp here:

NY 368573

Boomby Lane camps overlook the Wall and vallum and the two camps close to each other suggest a popular stopping point.

These sites are halfway between Burgh by Sands, the walker's target for the day, and Carlisle.

After some field research, the walker should head along the National Trail to Kirkandrews on Eden, where the Wall, trail and vallum at last come together. Not for long: the Wall heads off to take charge of the coast, the vallum seeing Burgh by Sands in its sights heads straight for it and the present road does the same. The National Trail is a more pleasant environment than the road so it is an enjoyable stroll along the edge of the river until Beaumont is reached. There are earthworks to the walker's left; these are the remains of the Carlisle ship canal, built just in time to see the coming of the railway and its conversion to one. The railway was equally unsuccessful, as the port of Silloth further south proved a more suitable spot for shipping – a point not lost on the author, as the walker will find out anon.

Burgh by Sands (Aballava) is reached and a delightful spot it is. The fort is straddling the modern road at the church; it is possible to work out the

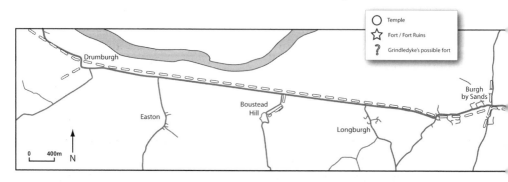

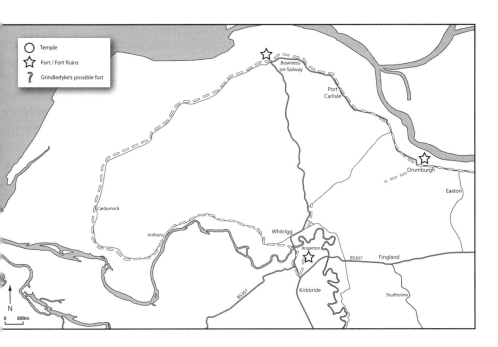

fort shape if you take the present boundaries on both sides of the road into account. The northern side of the fort is of particular importance as this faces a marsh with an easy crossing point from the northern side of the Solway. Enterprising tribes would undoubtedly have understood the opportunities and the Romans the need to keep such enthusiasm under control. Have a look for the hippo and the elephant at the church.

The fort is not the first military establishment in Burgh by Sands; there was a large wooden fort doing exactly the same job. This appears to have been extant at the time Hadrian made the decision to build a wall.

The entire way from Willowford to here started as a turf wall then all converted to stone, and the number of temporary construction camps along the way, especially on this stretch, indicates the scale of the numbers of personnel involved. Many were no doubt merely making their way through to other spots; some busy with the conversion from turf and palisade to stone, with the added exertion of the import of stone for the job. The military way would have been clogged with construction traffic; add to this delay in deliveries (due to the weather) the quantity of fodder and extra food for the troops. No small task, no small administration.

The movement of stone is of interest to the author; he holds the opinion that the desire for conversion to stone from turf put a considerable strain on the Roman military and the generals were able to justify the turf wall, palisade and ditch with milecastles and turrets remaining beyond Bowness-on-Solway to Ravenglass. Not because the army was under pressure from the enemy, but because of the necessity of transport by sea from the best western quarries around St Bees interfered with grain carrying and commerce. Grain was a necessity and commerce equalled taxes, plus the distances required: it simply wasn't worth the effort.

Refreshment can be found at:

The Greyhound Inn
Burgh by Sands
Carlisle
Cumbria CA5 6AN
Tel: 01228 576 579

Accommodation
www.rosemountcottage.co.uk

Hillside Farm
Boustead Hill
Burgh by Sands
Cumbria CA5 6AA
Tel: 01228 576 398
Web: www.hadrianswalkbnb.co.uk
Email: ruddshillside1@btinternet.com

This will put you a tad further on, ready for the morrow. The village is on the site of a pre-Roman (as far back as the Mesolithic) and Roman settlement.

Transportation back to Carlisle can be found at the bus stop near the church. Buses are becoming rarer; in fact, the author suspects that within a few years they will be in Tullie House Museum, the species having died out. If the walker cannot get local accommodation, this is about the last point from which a reasonably priced taxi fare can be considered.

Those staying the night can enjoy the walks down to the Solway and view the Edward I memorial. The author feels certain that there are a number of turrets, possibly pre-dating the Wall, dotted along this low-lying coastline – the need for obvious presence to make any invading force think twice because their preparation can be seen is a jolly good idea. Of a summer evening there is no better spot to watch birds and simply drink in the peace and quiet, away from absolutely everything; a single wader plodding along is noise enough.

Explore: there are plenty of byways. Indeed, if you wander around enough you may find there is considerably more to Burgh by Sands than originally thought. Certainly the number and size of Roman camps should keep the walker busy.

The walker may wish to stride on; to allow for the last day to include a return to Carlisle and journey home. The going is good and as long as there is daylight and a bed for the night arranged there is still more to see. See Day 10 for accommodation and travel.

Allowing for thorough exploration, the walker has managed roughly 13km today.

DAY 9

DAY 10

BURGH BY SANDS TO KIRKBRIDE

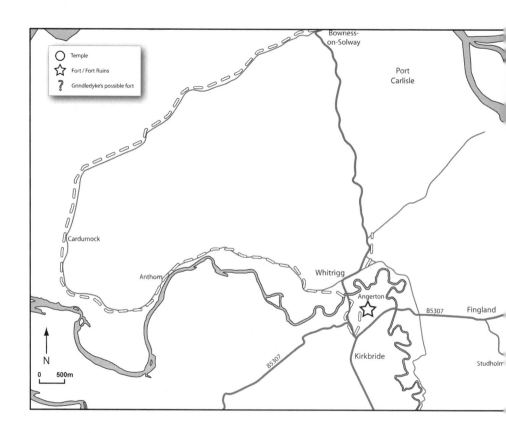

- Start at 9 a.m. at the latest
- Boots needed
- Terrain: good-going, tarmac all the way
- Beware exposed sections and tidal flooding
- A taxi may be needed to get you back to Carlisle
- There are very few buses from Kirkbride

Head westward along the National Trail towards Watch Hill, close to the site of milecastle 73, along the appropriate Dykesfield as the vallum is to the left, except it is the abandoned railway line to Port Carlisle. The past can be confusing.

The walker is instantly aware that they are on low-lying ground, Burgh Marsh. Building anything across this marsh would have taken considerable fortitude and skill; the area floods regularly – indeed, the signs helpfully inform the motorist and walker how deep the water can be. The Romans noted this factor and dispensed with any idea of a vallum, as a canal obviously was not the object of the exercise. The author is convinced that the Wall is sitting not only on the turf foundation, but the earliest Roman works here; they deliberately block a potential seaborne landing ground. It is not the case that the Romans expected a massive armada to turn up, but because it was Roman military practice: fastest route between two spots, straight, open beach line that the enemy can use – physically block it.

The vallum only reappears at the far end of the marsh at Drumburgh (Concavata) fort, NY264597. Unless the walker particularly enjoys front lawns

45 Burgh by Sands Church. Compare to the Warden Church tower on page 95

and bungalows, there is nothing to see. Excavations have revealed another civil-engineering oddity here: the Wall widens out to 3m. For how long is unclear; further archaeology is required. One thing is certain, the fort is not actually part of the Wall; it is detached and there are some academics that discount it as part of the frontier works at all, which the author thinks unfair as Castlesteads and Vindolanda are not attached, nor Arbeia, yet all three are considered integral to the picture of administrative control.

Drumburgh castle is a typical Cumbrian fortified house; typical in the sense that it is a fortified farmhouse – it's actually a well-loved home that has survived from the days of the reivers, those jolly enthusiastic cattle rustlers that took advantage of the fact that the lands between England and Scotland were debatable and thus lawless. This is a private residence, so please respect that fact. It contains some very fine stonework; no doubt the reivers appreciated it as they were trying to steal the owner's cattle. Note the garden ornaments.

Drumburgh Moss is also one of Cumbria Wildlife Trust's sites in the area.

Cumbria Wildlife Trust
www.cumbriawildlifetrust.org.uk

The road from Drumburgh to Glasson is not the best and the National Trail wisely takes a detour, which passes the course of the vallum: in Glasson turn left along the vallum. However, the walker should stop and consider some refreshment before leaving the spot as Glasson is worth spending a little time in, especially the Highland Laddie Inn. The food is grand and the walker should expect to be somewhat heavier upon the leaving. Ask about Haffnetting. The bridge over the canal is noteworthy; it is a shame the course is now utterly destroyed to the east.

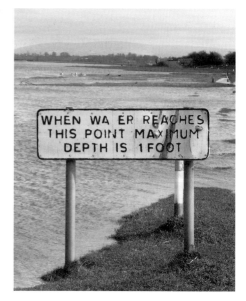

46 'You have been warned!'

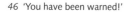

Highland Laddie Inn
www.highlandladdieinn.co.uk

Be aware that these low-lying sections can be extremely challenging in poor conditions and on occasions the sea likes to join in. The National Trail does a quick right to left and breaks free of the vallum and, for a change, takes the Wall itself as its base.

Port Carlisle is soon reached and the sorry remains of the sea lock for the canal are in view. Port Carlisle, or Fisher's Cross as it was until the ambitions of the canal company saw the need to change the name, offered a fording point to the northern shore of the Solway. Port Carlisle always had nature against it; silt in particular, and tides that, enraged by seasonal river flow, could prevent access for days.

These fording points across the wide but relatively shallow Solway would have proved a considerable problem for the Romans; the author suspects mostly from a tax avoidance and smuggling perspective, rather than an outright military offensive. Like all people that place themselves permanently by waters and gain their living from them, they entered into a special relationship, a day-to-day experience that builds into not just a lifetime, but an age, with cumulative experience and failure passed on over the generations. Any temporary military personnel would never have stood a chance in understanding the ripples, waves and mud that make up this coast and would have always been behind in any chase. Intimate understanding of the landscape is the thing and always will be.

Cattle were often taken across the waters; such valuable stock required management. The walker will have noticed tracks heading towards the Solway edge along the way which seem to have little obvious purpose.

Hope & Anchor Inn
www.hopeandanchorinn.com

Port Carlisle B&B
www.heskethouse.com

The vallum is now over to the left and the huddle of houses in the near distance is Bowness-on-Solway. Hadrian's Wall crosses in front of the walker at the start of the ascent into the village; like Wallsend, the Wall ends in the water.

Bowness-on-Solway (Maia) is in front of you. The walker may notice there is very little obviously Roman here to see. A small village clinging on to a

DAY 10

lump of high ground, looking out expectantly into the wide blue sea; the word charm is applicable, but without the chintz. The village facilities are a tad thin on the ground, but fortunately the Kings Arms survives and flourishes. There is an interpretation board to explain about Maia. If it wasn't there would anybody know that Bowness had such an illustrious past? See: www. english-heritage.org.uk/professional/research/landscapes-and-areas/national-mapping-programme/hadrians-wall-nmp/hadrians-wall-the-solway.

The contrast between the handling of the accepted terminus (or start) of the Wall could not be greater between Wallsend and Bowness-on-Solway. The major problem is, of course, that Maia for the most part lies under buildings which are unlikely to be cleared away in the near future. Archaeology has been undertaken, which, considering the difficulty of the site, is a chink of light in the darkness. The author believes much could be made of the large *vicus* to the east; the public are as interested in the day-to-day life of those on the Wall as they are of the Wall itself.

More needs to be done to provide the public with a better understanding of the sense of place at Bowness-on-Solway. Fortunately, the local population is rightly taking advantage of the Wall; slowly but surely tourism is providing a steady income and possibilities for the future. See www.britarch.ac.uk/lahs/Contrebis/2-39-Potter.pdf.

The walker should seek out a place of warmth and comfort.

Kings Arms
www.kingsarmsbowness.co.uk

Accommodation
www.maia-lodge.co.uk
www.wallsend.net
www.shoregatehouse.co.uk
www.oldchapelbownessonsolway.com

The good people of Bowness are justly proud of their status of being the start or finish of Hadrian's Wall; there is, of course, the point that they may be the end of the Wall, but they are just about halfway in respect of the Roman frontier. Being halfway is a justifiable thing to be proud of and well done them, as the pleasure gardens called the Banks are a genuine delight. Follow the signs and enjoy the view. The garden is a good meeting point, other than the pub, to pass the time with fellow walkers, starting or finishing their walk. No doubt some will be surprised that you are not finishing at Bowness and that you started at Tynemouth. The author would appreciate if you would spread the word. The walker can pride themselves in venturing where few have done before and are part of the process of understanding the past.

The gateway and mosaic are picturesque and quintessentially English in scale. Hadrian would have enjoyed the garden, but would be looking for a more imperial display.

This brings the author neatly to the point regarding Bowness: its position overlooking the mouth of the Solway is an excellent one, ideal for a bit of imperial showing off with the odd temple and statue to the goddess Maia, daughter of Atlas and Pleione, mother of Mercury by Jupiter, and of course a statue to Hadrian to be associated with it. You don't get anymore important than Jupiter in the Roman gods stakes and Hadrian, understanding the power of imagery, would see this as appropriate. No sign of such monument to imperial glory has been found. There may well be a reason; it might be elsewhere.

Another fascinating factor regarding Maia is that it appears to have been an after thought; it was not part of the original plan. The demolition of a milecastle to build it confirms that it was not considered necessary as part of the master plan. There is considerable academic debate in respect to what is and what is not part of the Wall from Carlisle to Bowness-on-Solway, much of which really does not assist the walker in enjoying the route. However, there is nothing wrong with a healthy dose of suspicion and enquiry. Maia appears to be a terminus of systems, the western frontier up from Ravenglass and the one from Wallsend – all very neat, but the author is pretty convinced that the Romans didn't look at it like this. It is quite probable that the important administrative centre was at Kirkbride, a short and near-equal distance to the south from Drumburgh Concavata. Maia is out on a limb, sitting above a very damp bit of coast and next to an ever-shallowing bay to the south (Cardunnock), as well as the bogs and gently raising mires. It is a peninsula and the weather could easily sever all communication; not necessarily an effective frontier defence as it at first may appear. Indeed, everything beyond Burgh by Sands is on the very margin, just above the ever-present weather and tide. There is the opportunity for crop growing and life outside the forts, but none of these forts beyond Burgh by Sands can possibly have been seen as great postings for the troops. However, it is a large fort, suggesting plenty of military activity, or potentially built large to make sure their neighbours to the north were fully aware of the power of the Roman presence. The only sensible role for the fort is enforcing tax and customs operating a 'stop-and-search' role, reliant upon small craft manned by experienced naval personnel. Alas, to date no inscriptions from Maia have provided such a link. However, the author is not deterred. Nor is he taking any of the shine off the effort to build Maia – at 2.8ha it is impressive. The only thing that particularly worries him is that for such a very large fort is the very small *vicus*. Now this could be the fact that no proper survey has been undertaken and that there is an extensive civilian settlement hidden from view, or that there simply isn't one – that would be extremely telling. More archaeology and resistivity is required to answer this! The author puts his money on there not being a big *vicus*.

The walker will have noticed that there is nothing of the fort to see, but with the skills learnt over the last few days will be able to note its edges, slight gradients off the platform in the east and south, and the steeper grade up from the Wall and the sheer cliff to the west. The one obvious feature is that Maia is not the place for a major port. The Wall blocks it to the north and the west is not practical. Like Tynemouth Priory, Bowness-on-Solway would provide an easily recognised maritime focal point; here is the edge of the Roman Empire standing out into the waves, a show of power, of unified organisation.

The walker, having refreshed at the pub, should now head south along the road towards Cardunnock. Walk off the fort platform by the first field gate to the left; proceed to Bowness-on-Solway primary school and down the bank to the bus turning circle, which doubles as a small official car park. This does not go down well with the bus drivers when the car drivers decide to expand their territory into that of the buses. However, this conflict is infrequent as the number of buses is not great and in a sense provides a modern equivalent of the fact that Bowness-on-Solway is isolated from everywhere. The author muses at the soldier watching the last wagon heading for Luguvalium of an evening, wishing he was on it, heading for a night out in the big city.

This area at the bottom of the slope would make a reasonable landing ground for a small harbour facility. This poses the question, is the south-facing gateway on the western (outside) side of the vallum and palisade, which is merrily heading for its first turret and milecastle, or is it on the inside and thus preventing access at this point from the beach? How the turf and wooden palisade connected to the stone fort is also of interest. The only way to find out is to re-excavate and see.

No doubt the walker would rightly assume that the exact position and sequence is known. Truthfully, the author is not convinced by the work so far undertaken that he can offer a definitive answer, nor frankly can anyone else. The walker should read the attached for what details we have, especially in respect of the southern gate: www.pastscape.org/hob.aspx?hob_id=10116.

The frontier defences are above on the left, keeping to the high ground. The presence of such a defence was first suggested in the late nineteenth century but not seriously considered until the 1930s; from then on archaeological excavation has slowly unearthed a frontier between Bowness-on-Solway and Ravenglass. There is no Wall; this is a turf-banked palisade and ditch with turrets and milecastles – much as the Wall was between Bowness and Willowford before rebuilding with stone. Towers start in wood and are rebuilt, in some cases more than once, in stone. The stone buildings along the way stayed in use until at least AD 290.

Academic Battlefield Ahead

The frontier is still patchy beyond Maryport and many academics believed that it simply did not exist, relying on the forts to respond rapidly to any insurgency or more likely tax avoidance and thus assuming a Trajanic way of dealing with administering a frontier. The author has spent many years considering this theory and has punched a few holes in it, based on the presence of a series of turret mounds between Ravenglass and Moresby fort at Whitehaven, south of Maryport. This work has included previously unrecognised Roman infrastructure along the way.

Academics and archaeologists have offered different numbers for the turret sequence, so the author is avoiding them; it has to be said that even he cannot quite understand the logic of 'Turret 0A and Turret 0B' – it somewhat undermines how the rest are sequenced if nobody can agree where '1' is.

A very reasonable synopsis is available here: www.dur.ac.uk/resources/ archaeological.services/research_training/hadrianswall_research_framework/ project_documents/Cumberland2.pdf.

The walker should ignore all this: the road is good walking and the Solway coast is simply breathtaking, especially at sundown. The whole area is an Area of Outstanding Natural Beauty, which comes as no surprise to anyone.

▌ Solway Coast AONB
www.solwaycoastaonb.org.uk

The frontier will stay on the walker's left for a good while. The first significant man-made feature to appear is the remains of the Solway viaduct, a lost Victorian railway triumph connecting England and Scotland in an attempt to save the cost of running coal trains through the railway hub at Carlisle. It was opened in 1869, closed in 1921 and demolished in 1934 to stop the Scots from drowning on Sunday, having enjoyed a pint on the English side.

DAY 10

47 Heavy skies over the remains of the Solway viaduct

It is subject of reuse as the site for a tidal energy scheme; it appears to be an ideal setting, although the author wonders if the promoters have taken into account the ice flows in the winter, which have severely damaged the viaduct in the past.

Up and over the old railway bridge and a quick look down to Bowness-on-Solway railway station, now a private residence and kept in very good order.

After the railway, the first field to the left contains a solitary altar stone. Whether it had been dropped on the way for post-Roman use as building material is unclear, but considering the weight of an altar stone, it does suggest that the military service road along the ditch, connecting the turrets and milecastles, was possibly intact after abandonment.

Milecastle 1 is in the field in to the left of Bigland House. The author has sympathy with the Roman incumbents of this milecastle. Consider being posted so close to the comfort of Maia, the bars and bathhouse all within very easy reach – being stuck in a windy milecastle is no fun.

Check your maps for a spot rather usefully called Campfield. There are three tower bases here which indicates the frontier system is well maintained and a certain amount of rigidity in the system. With the Solway flow and coastal drift, some of the turrets and milecastles could find themselves some distance from the best field of observation. The Wall manages to adjust where required; the frontier stays solidly on a surveyor's numeric rule.

The view of the Solway is and will continue to delight. The road is not very wide, but there is a wide verge. The walker is likely to see more cycles and tractors than cars. The road is gated to stop the cows popping into Bowness-on-Solway for a change of scenery; please close them as you go.

There are few obvious signs of the frontier: the bank to the left has melted away and the landmass is now flat on either side. To the left is the entrance to Cumbria Wildlife Trust's second reserve along the way.

The Solway mosses are spectacular and growing by the year. The railway crossing of the moss was more difficult to maintain than building the bridge over the Solway and continued to be so until the line was closed.

From Herd Hill the peninsula begins the turn south; the walker begins to feel a change in the wind on the face. For the turret and milecastle number crunchers there are a quantity of numbers and letters along this stretch. Quite simply the replacement and moving of wooden turrets, or tower in one instance, is the result of the timber rotting in the damp ground; the rigidity in the plan meant structures were sighted in horrible conditions with the obvious wet result.

At Vindolanda, the walker may have seen the reconstruction of a wooden fort; this assists in calculating the speed of deterioration of such structures. Based on the location, these wooden towers were replaced every five to seven years and re-sited, because of changes in the coastal landmass.

An interesting feature of the system is the milecastles are turf and wood built; the towers only are stone built. Why, nobody knows – yet. Any ideas? The author is always open to suggestions and theories.

The milecastle at Herd Hill (4) must have been an interesting place. It has a cemetery nearby and this makes the author wonder about the management of this frontier: the troops burying their comrades alongside the road within a glimpse of the sea that could take their spirits home; a lonely spot, but not a lost place, part of a great empire, where the dead were to be remembered right next to the living. It seems appropriate that the soldiers kept an eternal faith with each other. However, on stormy winter's nights, this unity may have been stretched a little; the ghosts of the dead too close for comfort. It is part of Roman burial and cremation practice to seek to be remembered; the worst of things was to be forgotten. Life for the Romans was one long ritual to ensure the personal balance was always tipped towards survival and acquiring remembrance. Joining one of the mystery cults, such as that of Mithras, was a way of attaining somewhere after in the afterlife whilst still alive. The initiate started the process of attaining credibility with the gods whilst alive, by carrying out rituals; the individual was enhancing, protecting and justifying themselves for the journey into death. This is particularly relevant when the individual finds themselves in an alien environment, such as a windy damp outpost such as Herd Hill. Barely above sea level, it would have been a very rough spot on a cold, wet January night, the waves crashing a short distance away, the wind howling and the horizontal rain drenching through every bit of clothing as the soldiers grimly stood guard looking out across a jet black sea. The ritual of the living and departed would have been in very close company here.

The author believes this milecastle had a reputation and further archaeological investigation is needed, especially for an associated religious site which may be so located to placate the gods that inhabited this spot. Managing his particular piece of frontier not only required the day-to-day maintenance of such a structure, but inclusion of the gods that existed along its length. This is equally the case for the Wall itself; there is no division in the Roman mind between the needs of engineering and military practicalities and the need to take the gods into consideration. It is even possible that some structures are deliberately sighted or moved either to placate or avoid causing offence (and thus ill fortune) to the builders and users.

The walker should not linger, lest the spirits decide to follow; stride out along the straight road which keeps roughly to the military supply route and Cardunnock is soon reached – a small hamlet that keeps low against the windy blast. This is a very small rural spot with some very ancient buildings if you seek them out. The author feels certain that the present road at Cardunnock is relatively modern as the village is on a slightly more westerly alignment, on top of the actual frontier. There are also some odd earthworks beyond the village pond that are worthy of further investigation. The author is convinced that the frontier headed inland at this point (milecastle 5 being on a peninsula) to avoid the bay that eventually became HMS *Nuthatch*.

The author will now mention the masts, the source of the UK time signals, sitting on the remains of the runways of HMS *Nuthatch*. As the present road bears right, one of the entrances to the base is on the left. In the field on the right is milecastle 5, which is bigger than those previously visited; the walker will note there is nothing to see, so will have to take the author's word for it. The masts will no doubt be taking the walkers attention anyway. The perimeter road can be hard going in wet weather; the gorse is a welcome wind break.

For those interested in airfield archaeology there are the remains of various concrete buildings which the cows thoroughly enjoy. Not one sign of a turret or milecastle is recorded beyond number 5. The system becomes conjectural; theory takes over and the walker is walking in a pretty vacuum as they enter the estuary of the Wampool River and the village of Anthorn is reached. The main gates of the base are on the left; a lonely, lost spot but a reasonably secure one, so no research beyond the fence line!

Anthorn, a pretty little spot overlooking the estuary, where the buildings indicate a flourish of agricultural interest on the coast in the eighteenth century, complete with a smart little Victorian tin chapel.

The walker will note that there is a track running slightly inland from the road they are upon; it curves away to the north-west and the line is cut by the airfield. This track provides a bit of shape to the area; Anthorn sits on the first bit of land in a very long time that could be described as safe from the waves. The airfield sits on the very flat bit. From milecastle 5 to Anthorn the airfield not only looks like a large pond, but the author thinks it is. To be precise a very shallow bay, which would put milecastle 5 on a peninsula; that being the case the next milecastle in the sequence is not following the present coastline, but inland towards the back of the airfield and the next roughly where St Mary's Tower stands today, taking the high ground, as the milecastles and turrets do at the beginning of the sequence at Bowness-on-Solway. Archaeologists have all looked along the coastal fringe up to now because the landscape sequence has drawn them rightly down to it; the problem is that they haven't considered going back up the grade when the opportunity arose.

March on past the modern version of a *vicus* – the smart, uniform estate of well-built homes for service families – and out again on to the flat land. From Anthorn the road gets busier again, so take care on this stretch. The remains of the railway bridge over the Wampool on the right and left the reduced remains of the road bridge which is the line of the track the walker has seen just outside Bowness; the railway having taken the straight line, but at a very large engineering cost. The walker will note the land is very flat and the slope to the left is an ancient beach line. The walker should continue straight on over the junction with the road to Kirkbride. Not over the bridge yet!

Note the area around Whitrigg Grange Farm and Whitrigg House; the archaeologist is very interested in is area: aerial photographs, taken over a period of years, at different times and in different conditions, indicate evidence of a series of anomalies in this area. Note the word anomaly; that is what any such finding remains until somebody puts a trowel in the ground and finds out for sure. It does appear that there is something here that might assist in our better understanding of the frontier, and especially the Roman control of the Wampool estuary. There is undoubtedly an ancient safe harbour with good communications not only north, but east towards the fort and *vicus* at Old Carlisle (Maglona).

Roman grain carriers either required deep-water ports or 'hards' to allow them to come to rest on stable ground. The Wall required vast amounts of material to build and service. This location is an ideal spot for sailing craft to come to rest, much better than Bowness-on-Solway, as it is sheltered and has potential deep water even at low tide. The author is convinced that the rivers and estuaries played a vital part in the supply to the Wall on both east and west coasts. Primarily stone (especially in the west) for construction of the Wall, foodstuffs, general trade goods, horses and troops are all quicker and in some cases safer transported by sea than bounced along or clogging the roads.

Turn right at the junction with Whitrigg House on the left. A few metres along this road and a Roman road crosses the walker's path at a 70-degree angle to the fence line. It is easy to find as it jumps out of the landscape and points directly across the estuary to a barn; straight at the Roman fort of Kirkbride. Very close to this point a ferry service must have operated; such a service would have required management, administration and services for those waiting to cross. Allowing for the passing of time and silt, it is possible to work out the outline of a small port facility here. Especially when the walker turns right at the end of the short road and heads back towards Anthorn. There is evidence of a later fording point immediately off the road to the left at the junction.

This is one estuary that the Romans would not cross with a bridge. A chain ferry seems the likeliest, with large, flat-bottomed, punt-like craft capable of carrying 30 horses (examples of such craft have been found on the Rhine). There is a very sensible landing ground at the foot of the bank on the Kirkbride side of the river.

There is evidence of a Roman road heading south from Bowness-on-Solway and it appears to be heading towards the very same spot. It would make sense for the main road to go via the fort at Kirkbride (and possibly at Whitrigg Farm) to Bowness-on-Solway via the inland route; it is shorter and avoids the large shallow bay where the airfield is today.

Warning this area is prone to flooding in high tides.

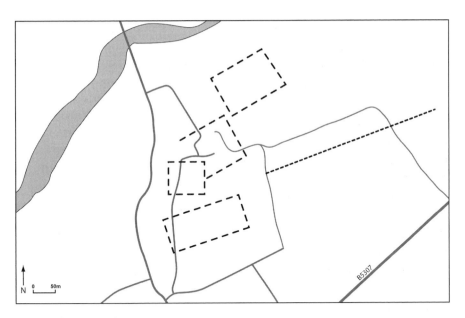

48 Kirkbride fort anomalies

Turn left at the junction for Kirkbride; over the narrow Wampool Bridge. Don't linger on the bridge; this is quite a busy stretch. Do linger, if safe to do so, when across: the view is wonderful, especially when the tide is in. Looking back across the Wampool it is obvious the ridge across the way is ideal for turrets. It would be easy to control this estuary on either side.

Welcome to Kirkbride, a charming spot with more facilities than most in the area and, most importantly, a Roman fort. Beware the road which is quite busy and head off the bridge towards an unmarked footpath on the left between two hedges. This dark little path takes you up a steep bank directly to St Bridget's church.

The author more than suspects that this little path actually goes straight through the western gates of one of the forts on this site – more work needs to be done!

St Bridget's is truly a delightful place to end the journey, so please support the upkeep of this truly charming church, which sits very prominently on top of a well-constructed north-to-south playing-card-shaped platform. But it is not the only one; there appears to be another running east–west covering the southern end of the north–south platform and another square–shaped anomaly in the field to the north-east, directly above the steep-sloped edge of the estuary; which the author has noted

DAY 10

Left: 49 The unmarked way up to St Bridgets

Below: 50 St Bridgets, Kirkbride

from aerial photographs. All this comes as no surprise as this site is most probably *Portus Trucculensis*, but there again, that title maybe assigned to Whitriggs across the estuary near the Roman road, as ports tend not to be on top of banks. The important fact is that you, the walker, have acknowledged this fort is here. It is; a hole has been dug and the physical remains viewed, if only briefly, but it is enough to start with. More, of course, needs to be done.

Is this the spot where the Roman military supply of Black Burnished Ware pottery came ashore, all the way from the Dorset coast; the pottery much favoured by the soldiers along the Wall from the second to the fourth century?

Take a walk along the lane heading around the boundary of the church on to the footpath through the farm which brings you to the outlook towards Whitriggs; the square-shaped anomaly lies in the lower part of the field, though nothing can be seen on the surface. Take the path on the right through the wicket gate and then look back towards the church; the old vicarage wall line gives you an indication of the edge of one platform. However, it is not alone; the path, which is very well kept, trundles over a pretty significant hump. This may be the Roman road heading east towards Carlisle, avoiding the military way along the frontier. The path takes the walker to a junction where a right-hand turn on to Birch Hill Lane should be taken; note the false horizon on the field to the right. The walker will have circumnavigated the area of archaeological study when they reach the junction with Church Road. Fortunately, archaeology has proved at least one fort site here, but there is an awful lot more to be done – at least a proper start has been made!

Let us review what the walker has achieved. A very long walk, full of adventures and asides; it will have included everything that nature can throw, chuck, blow and fire at them. The boots will have lost a good deal of tread. But the walker will have discovered, seen, considered, noted, puzzled and wondered why they are doing this, and then understood why. The reality is that the walker has entered into a pact with the landscape; like the man on the bicycle or the old man and his dog, they have passed through a land, experienced it, lived it, left their tracks and moved on. This guide has not been a case of seeing the route through the author's eyes; it is the walker responding to the whole. The author hopes that he has supplied enough to fuel a personal response. There is the need to keep moving along; the Wall, the route, the environment, draws the walker in, the act of walking through it actually affects the way the landscape is perceived.

DAY 10

The perception of the walker towards the Wall, its physical remains and its absence, will have changed from those first moments at Tynemouth. The walker has all the pieces and the author need not say more; the walker can make their own mind up as to the evidence.

Whilst it is possible to do the walk in five days, what would have been missed? The last 12km are in an unknown land where the past is still waiting to be discovered. Unlike the rest of the Wall this is not well interpreted, it is still rough around the edges and worthy of more public attention. By walking this route both the gap between Tynemouth and Wallsend, and our understanding of the Cumbrian coast, are brought to the public consciousness.

Kirkbride offers a terminus along a part of the Hadrianic system that was never converted from turf to stone; it is thus a remnant of the original Hadrianic plan. It has a harbour facility and at least one protecting fort (quite possibly two) from which it has fast communication routes to Bowness-on-Solway and possibly Burgh by Sands to the north. In this respect it is a better representation of the Hadrianic frontier than that so far found at Tynemouth. There is actual evidence of a frontier system beyond the stone wall, and these are actual parts, not additions to it.

The western frontier is quite honestly not understood; it was constructed during Hadrian's reign and was never converted to stone, save for its milecastle and forts; it cannot be treated as different as it is part of the overall frontier system. The idea of limiting the territory occupied is even more extreme when it faces the sea and the Isle of Man and Ireland. The Wall has forward bases beyond, such as Bewcastle; no such opportunity to the west.

By walking beyond the accepted start and finish points, and walking from the east to the west, the walker is offering up opportunities for others; for public support for further archaeological research, and also for the local economies of Tynemouth, Kirkbride and Anthorn. These areas have not fully benefitted from the Hadrian's Wall tourism boost, and they deserve to because they are part of it. The author has done his bit by producing the book *Walking Hadrian's Coastal Way – Ravenglass to Bowness-on-Solway*, which is available from all good bookshops.

This is the end of the walk. Fortunately there is a pub near at hand.

The walker has travelled roughly 20km today.

Bush Inn
Kirkbride
Kirkbride
Wigton CA7 5HT
Tel: 01697 351 694

There is limited public transport here, and the easiest way back to Carlisle is via Wigton. There are reasonable rail and bus services from the town.

Taxis
Station House 01697 343 148
Able Taxis 01697 731 508
Town Village Link 01697 344 527

VERY WELL DONE!

51 What it's all about – wide open spaces

DAY 10

USEFUL LIST

For Emergencies
Emergency services: police, ambulance, fire dial 999.

Identify the service you require; when connected provide your name, location and what service is required and why. The emergency services do not provide directions if you get lost. That is why you have a compass and a map.

Non-life-threatening medical accident & emergencies:

Web: www.nhsdirect.nhs.uk

Tel: 0845 4647

Used to find doctors, dentists, pharmacies, accident & emergency departments.

Transport
National Rail enquiries: www.nationalrail.co.uk

Local Trains: At the time of publication, Northern Rail operate the Newcastle to Carlisle service and the coastal service to Wigton, Maryport, Whitehaven and Ravenglass. It should be noted that the connection between the two services at Carlisle is utterly appalling.

Bus & Other Transport: www.transportdirect.info

Preparing for the Walk
Tourist Information Centres:

Newcastle
8–9 Central Arcade
Newcastle-upon-Tyne
Tel: 0191 277 8000

Carlisle
Carlisle Old Town Hall
Green Market
Carlisle
Tel: 01228 625 600

Boot & Kit Shops:
The author always recommends walking-in a pair of boots prior to beginning a big walk; if you find you have a problem these outlets ought to be able to help. It is essential to be perfectly comfortable with your footwear before you commence this walk.

LD Mountain Centre
34 Dean Street
Newcastle-upon-Tyne
Tyne and Wear
Tel: 0191 232 3561
Web: www.ldmountaincentre.com

Cotswold Outdoor
74–76 English Street
Carlisle
Tel: 01228 596 037
Web: www.cotswoldoutdoor.com

BIBLIOGRAPHY

Allason-Jones, L. (2001). 'The material culture of Hadrian's Wall', *Limes XVIII* – proceedings of the XVIIIth ICRFS Amman, Jordan, BAR S1084

Barnes, T.D. (1967). 'Hadrian and Lucius Verus', *Journal of Roman Studies*

Bellhouse, R. (1989). *Roman Sites on the Cumberland Coast: A new schedule of coastal sites*, CWAAS Research Series, Volume III

Bennett, J., (1980). " 'Temporary' camps along Hadrian's Wall", Hanson & Keppie (eds), *Roman Frontier Studies 1979*, 12th ICRFS, BAR International Series

Bidwell, P. (2003). 'The original eastern terminus of Hadrian's Wall', *Archaeologia Aeliana 32*

Biggins, J.A. & Taylor, D.J.A. (2004). 'A geophysical survey at Housesteads Roman Fort, April 2003', *Archaeologia Aeliana*

Birley, Anthony R. (1997). *Hadrian: The Restless Emperor*, London: Routledge

Birley, Eric B. (1961). *Research on Hadrian's Wall*, Titus Wilson & Son

Blair, Robert (1895). *Handbook to the Roman Wall* (4th edn), Society of Antiquaries of Newcastle-upon-Tyne

Breeze, David J. (1934), *Handbook to the Roman Wall* (14th revised edn, November 2006), Society of Antiquaries of Newcastle-upon-Tyne

Breeze, David J. & Dobson, Brian (1976). *Hadrian's Wall*, Allen Lane

Crow, J. (2004). *Housesteads: A Roman Fort on Hadrian's Wall*, Stroud

Daniels, Charles (1979). 'Review: Fact and Theory on Hadrian's Wall', *Britannia*

Greene, Kevin (1992). *Roman Pottery* (Interpreting the Past Series), University of California Press

Hodgson, N. (2000). 'The Stanegate: A Frontier Rehabilitated', *Britannia*

Horsley, John (1732). *Britannia Romana or the Roman Antiquities of Britain* (1974), Frank Graham

Hutton, William (1801). *The History of the Roman Wall: 1801*, University of Michigan Library

Johnson, Anne (1983). *Roman Forts of the 1st and 2nd centuries AD in Britain and the German Provinces*, London: Adam & Charles Black

Jones, G.D.B., (1976). 'The western extension of Hadrian's wall: Bowness to Cardurnock', *Britannia*

Simpson, F.G. (1931). 'Excavations on Hadrian's Wall between Heddon-on-the-Wall and North Tyne in 1930', *Archaeologia Aeliana*

Wilmott, Tony (2009). *Hadrian's Wall: Archaeological Research by English Heritage 1976–2000*, English Heritage

Wilmott, Tony (1997). *Birdoswald: Excavations of a Roman Fort on Hadrian's Wall and its Successor Settlements, 1987–92*, London

Woodfield, Charmian (1965). 'Six Turrets on Hadrian's Wall', *Archaeologia Aeliana*

Yourcenar, Marguerite (2005). *Memoirs of Hadrian*, New York: Farrar, Straus & Giroux

Websites

www.ads.ahds.ac.uk – Archaeological Data Service

www.gis1.cumbria.gov.uk – Cumbria County Council GIS

www.roman-britain.org – Roman Britain Organisation; the author believes this to be a very credible attempt at a national view of Roman activity in Britain; researched and operated by English Heritage.

Other Sources

Archaeology North: Council for British Archaeology Regional Group Three 8/1994/10

INDEX